CAMBRIDGE LIBRARY COLLECTION

Books of enduring scholarly value

Latin American Studies

This series focuses on colonial Latin America and the Caribbean. It includes historical and statistical reference works from the eighteenth and nineteenth centuries, reports describing scientific, archaeological and ethnological expeditions, and editions of accounts from the earliest period of European settlement.

A Treatise on Sugar

Benjamin Moseley (1742–1819) was an English doctor who left England and spent eighteen years working in Kingston, Jamaica. His time there coincided with the massive expansion of sugar production on the island. Drawing on his own experience as well as an extensive range of classical and contemporary published sources, Moseley presents a lively history of the cultivation and use of sugar cane. The work, first published in 1799 and expanded in this second edition in 1800, discusses the origins of the plant and its later cultivation and development in the Americas, as well as the popularity of refined sugar. Special attention is devoted to the plant's medicinal uses. Moseley also became known for his outspoken opposition to the growing practice of vaccination, and he uses a medical essay in the appendix of this book to launch an attack on the effectiveness of cowpox in inoculations.

Cambridge University Press has long been a pioneer in the reissuing of out-of-print titles from its own backlist, producing digital reprints of books that are still sought after by scholars and students but could not be reprinted economically using traditional technology. The Cambridge Library Collection extends this activity to a wider range of books which are still of importance to researchers and professionals, either for the source material they contain, or as landmarks in the history of their academic discipline.

Drawing from the world-renowned collections in the Cambridge University Library and other partner libraries, and guided by the advice of experts in each subject area, Cambridge University Press is using state-of-the-art scanning machines in its own Printing House to capture the content of each book selected for inclusion. The files are processed to give a consistently clear, crisp image, and the books finished to the high quality standard for which the Press is recognised around the world. The latest print-on-demand technology ensures that the books will remain available indefinitely, and that orders for single or multiple copies can quickly be supplied.

The Cambridge Library Collection brings back to life books of enduring scholarly value (including out-of-copyright works originally issued by other publishers) across a wide range of disciplines in the humanities and social sciences and in science and technology.

A Treatise on Sugar

Benjamin Moseley

CAMBRIDGE
UNIVERSITY PRESS

CAMBRIDGE UNIVERSITY PRESS

Cambridge, New York, Melbourne, Madrid, Cape Town,
Singapore, São Paolo, Delhi, Mexico City

Published in the United States of America by Cambridge University Press, New York

www.cambridge.org
Information on this title: www.cambridge.org/9781108050500

This edition first published 1800
This digitally printed version 2012

ISBN 978-1-108-05050-0 Paperback

A TREATISE ON SUGAR.

WITH

MISCELLANEOUS MEDICAL OBSERVATIONS.

BY

BENJAMIN MOSELEY, M. D.

AUTHOR OF A TREATISE ON

TROPICAL DISEASES;

MILITARY OPERATIONS;

AND THE

CLIMATE OF THE WEST INDIES;

AND

A TREATISE ON COFFEE:

PHYSICIAN TO CHELSEA HOSPITAL,

MEMBER OF THE COLLEGE OF PHYSICIANS OF LONDON,

OF THE UNIVERSITY OF LEYDEN,

OF THE AMERICAN PHILOSOPHICAL SOCIETY

AT PHILADELPHIA, &c. &c.

SECOND EDITION,

WITH CONSIDERABLE ADDITIONS.

LONDON:

PRINTED BY JOHN NICHOLS,

RED-LION PASSAGE, FLEET-STREET,

FOR G. G. AND J. ROBINSON, PATERNOSTER-ROW.

M DCCC.

PREFACE

TO THE

SECOND EDITION.

MY endeavour in the firſt edition, or rather ſketch of this work, to penetrate the denſe umbrage, which has ſo long enveloped the principal objects of my reſearch, has been favourably received by the public; and by thoſe individuals, who themſelves have laboured, without a pioneer, in the unfrequented receſſes of literature.

In this edition much new matter will be found; and I am not without hopes that ſome of it will be acceptable to the friends of ſcience, and to the promoters of public good.

In the republic of letters, it is admitted as a fundamental axiom, that every perſon has a right to treat a commodity he has purchaſed, as he pleaſes.—He may grumble, find fault, and abuſe; becauſe the rules of decency in this republic are equivocal; and there is no law to compel him to underſtand the object of his reſentment.

He may, if he chuſe, ſell an author by weight to the cheeſemonger; or conſign his brains to this, or any other more baſe and ignoble fate, for depreciating, in his opinion, the value of the paper on which they are diſplayed.

This cannot be prevented.—For, in this republic, Tom Fool, and Tom-a-Bedlam, will contend, that Francis Bacon, and Iſaac Newton, belong to the ſame God with themſelves;—

ſelves;—and that to wage war againſt ignorance, is to invade their province and chartered privileges.—I accord.—Were it not ſo, I ſhould have noticed one or two of theſe blundering, illiterate, purveyors of dullneſs, who took,—to the full extent of their rights,—liberties with the firſt edition of this publication.

Prompted by hunger, or directed by lunar influence, they acted, perhaps, againſt their conſcience; or in an irreſiſtible paroxyſm of mental derangement.

Candour has, beſides, another plea to advance in their favour.

On inquiry, I was informed who theſe deſperate academicians were; and that they have a phyſical protection againſt any attempt to alienate their minds, from their ferocious cuſtoms.—Their ſkulls, like thoſe of the Braſilian Indians, mentioned by PURCHAS, "are "as hard as the wood which grows in their "country,

" country, and cannot be broken; ſo that " their enemies may uſe their weapons on " them in vain. That hard-head, and block- " head, terms of reproach among rational " people, with them, are terms of honour, " and gentlemanlike qualifications."

B. M.

LONDON, Pall Mall,
1ſt of January, 1800.

SUGAR CANE.

Arundo Saccharifera.	C. Bauhin, *Pin.* 18.
Arundo Saccharina.	J. Bauhin, 2. 531.
Arundi Sacchari.	F. Hernandez, *p.* 109.
Calamus Saccharatus.	Munting, *Pl. Cult*, *p.* 284.
Cannæ Dulces.	P. Martyr.
Canna Mellea.	Cæsalpin, *Hiſt. Plant.* *p.* 182.
Canna Saccharifera.	Ogilby, *Chin.* I. 228.
Canna Saccharina.	Nieuhof, *p.* 89.
Canna Sacchari.	Laet, *lib.* I. *p.* 27.
Harundo Saccharifera.	Parkinson, *Theatr. Botan.* 1210.
Roſeaux, ou Cannes de Sucre.	Labat. *vol.* I. *p.* 228.
Roſeaux de Sucre.	Lussan.
Saccharum floribus paniculatis.	Lin. *Sp. Pl.*
Tacomaree, ſive Arunda Saccharifera.	Piso, *Lib.* IV. *Cap.* I.
Viba & Tacomareé & Canna Sacchari.	Ib.
Vubæ & Tacomareé Braſilienſibus.	Marcgrav, 82.

S U G A R.

K,hand. *Hindoostanee.*

شكّر سكّر, *Sukker, Shukker.* *Arabicè.*

شكر *Seker* *Persicè,* & *Turcicè.*

Μελι καλαμινον. THEOPHASTUS.

Σακχαρον. DIOSCORIDES.

Saccaron. PLINIUS.

Σακχαρι. Μελι καλαμινον. ARRIANUS.

Σακχαρ. GALENUS.

Αλς Ινδικος. P. ÆGINETA, *ab* ARCHIGENE.

Saccharum. *Latinè.*

Zuccharo. *Italicè.*

Açúcar. *Hispanicè.*

Sucre. *Gallicè.*

Zúcker. *Germanicè.*

Suycker. *Belgicè.*

HISTORY

HISTORY

OF THE

SUGAR CANE.

I HAVE undertaken a difficult taſk, in attempting to give an Hiſtory of SUGAR.

Much time has elapſed ſince the cultivation of the ſugar cane has been generally known, and ſugar in almoſt general uſe. Yet no perſon hitherto has connected any regular ſeries of facts on the ſubject; a ſubject of the firſt importance in commerce: and, more than that, a ſubject now influencing the diſpoſitions to health or diſeaſe, of the greater part of the inhabitants of the earth.

The materials which preſent themſelves for my purpoſe, are disjointed and contradictory. The rays, which ſcarcely illumine the ſurface of the maſs I am to penetrate, are feeble and confuſed. To diſcover a foundation, on which order and arrangement may riſe, I muſt toil through trackleſs regions of obſcurity.

The moſt antient author, who mentions the ſugar cane, is THEOPHRASTUS, who lived 321 years before the Chriſtian æra. I ſhall begin

 with

with him; and recite a few paſſages and alluſions from other authors, as they deſcend in point of time, which have been ſuppoſed relative to this plant.

THEOPHRASTUS ſays, in his chapter on honey,—

Οτι αι του μελιτος γενεσεις, τριτται· η απο των ανθων, και εν οις αλλοις εστιν η γλυκυτης· αλλη δε εκ του αερος, οταν αναχυθεν, υγρον απο του ηλιου συνεψηθεν πεση, γινεται δε τουτο μαλιστα υπο πυραμητον· αλλη δε εν τοις καλαμοις.*

"The generation of honey is threefold: the firſt ſort is from flowers, or other things in which there is ſweetneſs: the ſecond, from the air, which, when there are dews, is concocted by the heat of the ſun, and falls particularly in harveſt time: the third ſort is from canes or reeds."

He mentions that the ſecond ſort of honey, or that generated from the moiſture in the air, falls on the earth, and on plants; and is found chiefly on the boughs of the oak, and *Tilia*, or lime tree.

By the cane, which yields the third ſpecies of honcy, it is ſuppoſed that he implies the ſugar cane; and the honey, the juice, perhaps inſpiſſated, of that plant.

* Ed. HEINSII, 1613, p. 475.

THEO-

THEOPHRASTUS mentions another ſort of reed or cane, growing in marſhy places in Egypt, with ſweet roots. Speaking of the different properties of the different parts of plants, he ſays,—

—Καθαπερ εν Αιγυπτῳ του καλαμου του εν τοις ελεσιν· εχει μεν γαρ τινα γλυκυτητα και αλλως επι των ακρων, αλλ' επι βραχυ παντων. Εκεινος δε δια την ευτροφιαν απαλος γε επι πλειον εστι και γλυκυς. Εχουσι δε και αι ριζαι την γλυκυτητα μεχρις ου αν ξηρανθωσιν. Αναξηρανθεισαι δὲ ουκ-ετι, το γαρ ξηρον, ουτ' εδωδιμον, ουτ' εσχυλον *

"As in the reed that grows in moiſt places in Egypt; the extreme parts of which are alſo ſweet, though in a ſmall degree. But for the greater part, it is tender and ſweet, on account of the copious nouriſhment diffuſed through it. Even the roots are ſweet until they are dry; then they loſe their ſweetneſs, and are not proper for food, and are not ſavoury."

Whether THEOPHRASTUS, who was a Leſbian, had ever ſeen this reed in Egypt with ſweet roots, or whether he had the account of it from others, or whether ſuch a reed really

* De Cauſis Plant. lib. VI. c. 16. ed. HEINSII.

exifts, may be equally a matter of conjecture; but I have given his account of it, becaufe other writers have mentioned this reed with fweet roots, probably from him: and many have fuppofed the *Sugar Cane* was the reed alluded to, though erroneoufly defcribed. But this will be better underftood by comparing this paffage in THEOPHRASTUS, with what has been faid by other early writers.

VARRO (68 years before the Chriftian æra), in the following verfes, obferves,—

Indica non magna nimis arbore crefcit arundo;
Illius è lentis premitur radicibus humor,
Dulcia cui nequeant fucco contendere mella *.

"The Indian reed does not grow to a large tree; from its vifcid roots a liquor is preffed, to which honey cannot be compared for fweetnefs."

DIONYSIUS AFER (*anno* 3. Ær. Chr. SAX. *Onomaft.*) mentions that the Indians drink the juice of the Ερυθραιος καλαμος, or Indian cane †.

* VARRO Narbonenfis, or, as he is fometimes called, VARRO *Atacinus*, a poetical writer, contemporary with the celebrated M. T. VARRO.

† Periegefis, viz. 1127.

STRABO

STRABO *(anno* 19), in his 15th book of Geography, in the deſcription of India, ſays, on the authority of NEARCHUS (Alexander's admiral), who lived 325 years before the Chriſtian æra,—

Ειρηκε δε και περι των καλαμων οἱ ποιουσι μελι μελισσων μη ουσων· ου γαρ δενδρον ειναι καρποφορον· εκ δε του ΚΑΡΠΟΥ *μεθυειν* *.

"He (NEARCHUS) relates, that the reed (in India) yields honey without bees; but it is not a fruit-bearing tree: yet the *fruit* intoxicates."

The latter part of this paſſage has perplexed commentators.—Would ΟΠΟΥ remove the difficulty?

In the ſame page STRABO ſays, on the authority of ERATOSTHENES,—

Τας ριζας των φυτων και μαλιστα των μεγαλων καλαμων, γλυκειας και φυσει και εψησει.

"The roots of plants (in India), particularly of the great reeds, are ſweet by nature, and by decoction."

He alſo mentions the *καλαμος Ινδικος* growing abundantly in Æthiopia.

SENECA *(anno* 62) in his 84th Epiſtle, has the following paſſage:—

* P. 1016. edit. 1707.

Aiunt

Aiunt inveniri apud Indos mel in harundinum foliis; quod aut ros illius cœli, aut ipſius harundinis humor dulcis, et pinguior gignat. In noſtris quoque herbis vim eandem, ſed minus manifeſtam, & notabilem poni; quam proſequatur et contrahat animal huic rei genitum.

"They ſay that, in the Indies, honey is found on the leaves of canes; which is produced by the dew, or the ſweet juice of the cane itſelf, concreting. In our herbs alſo there is the ſame quality, but in a leſs degree; from which the bees extract honey."

This, being in the time of NERO, proves that the Romans, at that period, knew but little of the ſugar cane, and nothing of the manufacture of ſugar.

LUCAN *(anno* 62) ſays, in the 237th verſe of his third book, when ſpeaking of the Indians near the Ganges,—

Quique bibunt tenera dulces ab arundine ſuccos.

"They drink the ſweet juices of the tender reed."

PLINY *(anno* 78) in the 32d chapter of the 6th book, ſpeaking of the *Inſulæ Fortunatæ*, or or what are now called the Canary Iſlands, aſſerts, on the authority of *Juba*, that, in the iſland called *Ombrios*,—

Arbores ſimiles Ferulæ, ex quibus aqua exprimatur; ex nigris amara; ex candidioribus potui jucunda.

"There are trees reſembling the *Ferula*, from which water may be expreſſed; the water from the black ſort is bitter; but that from the white, grateful to drink."

SALMASIUS, GEOFFROY, and many other authors, have believed that theſe trees, mentioned by PLINY, were ſugar canes; but certainly without reaſon.

If we may credit the Spaniſh hiſtorian of theſe iſlands, there was in his time*, in the ſame iſland, now called *Ferro*†, or *Hierro*, a marvellous tree, which made up for the deficiency of ſprings, and contributed largely towards ſupplying the inhabitants of the iſland with water. Some writers conſider PLINY's remark applicable to this vegetable fountain, which is deſcribed as follows.

* In the year 1632.

† *Ferro* is about fifteen leagues in circumference, and five in breadth. It is ſubject to frequent droughts, there being only three inconſiderable ſprings in it.

"The

" The diſtrict in which this tree ſtands is called *Tigulahe*, near to which, and in the cliff or ſteep rocky aſcent that ſurrounds the whole iſland, is a narrow gutter or gully, which commences at the ſea, and continues to the ſummit of the cliff, where it joins or coincides with a valley, which is terminated by the ſteep front of a rock. On the top of this rock grows a tree, now called *Til*, but, in the language of the antient inhabitants, *Garſe*, i. e. Sacred, or Holy Tree. Its leaves conſtantly diſtil ſuch a quantity of water as is ſufficient to furniſh drink to every living creature in *Hierro*; Nature having provided this remedy for the drought of the iſland. On the North ſide of the trunk are two large tanks or ciſterns of rough ſtone, or rather one ciſtern divided, each being twenty feet ſquare, and ſixteen ſpans in depth. One of theſe contains water for the drinking of the inhabitants, and the other that which they uſe for their cattle, waſhing, and ſuch like purpoſes. Every morning, near this part of the iſland, a cloud or miſt ariſes from the ſea, which the South and Eaſterly winds force againſt the fore-mentioned ſteep cliff; ſo that the cloud, having no vent but by the gutter, gradually aſcends it, and from thence advances ſlowly to the extremity of the valley, where it it is ſtopped and checked by the front of the rock which terminates the valley, and then reſts upon the thick leaves and wide-ſpreading branches of the tree, from whence it diſtils in drops during the remainder of the day, until it is at length exhauſted, in the ſame manner that we ſee water drip from the leaves of trees after a heavy ſhower of rain.

"This diſtillation is not peculiar to the *Garſe*, or *Til*; for the *Breſos*, which grow near it, likewiſe drop water; but, their leaves being but few and narrow, the quantity is ſo trifling, that though the natives ſave ſome of it, yet they make little or no account of any but what diſtils from the *Til*.

"A perſon lives on the ſpot near which this tree grows, who is appointed by the council to take care of it and its water. He every day diſtributes to each family of the diſtrict ſeven pots or veſſels full of water, beſides what he gives to the principal people of the iſland*."

That ſome trees and ſhrubs may, on hydraulic principles, become ſyphons to the earth, and their extremities diſcharge a conſiderable quantity of water imbibed from the roots, is certainly poſſible; and ſuch trees are related

* GLASS's Hiſtory of the Canary Iſlands, p. 275, *anno* 1764.

by

by travellers to exiſt in Africa, and South America. But the hiſtory of the *Garſe* is ſcarcely within the compaſs of credibility. There may be ſome trees peculiar to *Ferro*, abounding with moiſture, which PLINY had heard of; and, on that account, I have introduced the preceding relation. Indeed, they are mentioned by ſeveral ſubſequent writers; particularly by PETER MARTYR, who ſays, "In the iſland of *Ferro* there is no other water that may be drunk, but only that is gathered of the dew which continually diſtilleth from one only tree, growing on the higheſt bank of the iſland, and falleth into a round trench made with man's hand." *Decad.* I. *Lib.* I. *anno* 1493.

STATIUS (*anno* 95), *Sylvarum*, *Lib.* 1. *ſub finem*, has a paſſage, which has been the foundation of much diſpute among critics and commentators; ſome contending that the reading ſhould be *cannæ*, canes; others, that it ſhould be *caunæ*, figs: ſo called from *Caunus*, a town in Egypt, famous for figs.

Et quas percoquit Ebuſia cannas *.

"The iſland of *Ebuſus* (or *Ivica*, in the Mediterranean, near Valencia in Spain), which produces ripe canes."

* *Et quod præcoquit Æbeſia cannas.* Ed. Veneta, 1475.

Et

Et quas percoquit Ebosea caunas.

"Ebusus which ripens *(caunæ)* figs."

Solinus *(anno* 218), in the 52d chapter of his Polyhistoria, in describing India, says,—

Quæ palustria sunt, arundinem creant ita crassam, ut fissis internodiis lembi vice vectitet navigantes; è radicibus ejus exprimitur humor dulcis ad melleam suavitatem *.

"The marshy places produce reeds so large, that between the joints, when divided in the middle, they are capable of carrying people in the manner of boats; from the roots of this reed a juice is expressed as sweet as honey."

Solinus has taken the first part of this passage from Pliny; who, as well as Herodotus, says, that the Indians make boats, or canoes, from canes growing in marshy places: but neither Herodotus nor Pliny mention the sweetness of their roots.

Herodotus, 444 years before the Christian æra, in his *Thalia*, says the Indians, who inhabit the morasses of the river, feed on raw fish, which they catch in boats made of reeds; a single joint of which is large enough for one boat: and Pliny, in the 2d chapter

* P. 275, edit. Goezii, 1777.

of his 7th book, ſays, in India the canes grow to ſo great a ſize, that, from a ſingle joint, a boat may be made capable of carrying three people.

I have now ſelected every thing, excepting the trivial common-place matter (which may be found in almoſt every Lexicon), reſpecting the *cane*, or *reed*, to which the property of *ſweetneſs* has been attributed, by every writer preceding the reign of prieſtcraft, ignorance, and oblivion. I ſhall paſs over that long night of human reaſon, where nothing is to be found,—to the more certain and determinate hiſtory of the ſugar cane.

On the diſcovery of the Weſtern hemiſphere, the Sugar Cane was found on the continent; and alſo in ſome of the Atlantic iſlands; but the art of making ſugar, it is ſaid, never was practiſed by the aborigines of the Weſt Indian iſlands, until they were ſettled by Europeans; nor by the Mexicans, or Peruvians, or any other native inhabitants of South America, previous to their ſubjugation by the Spaniards.

Of this there may be ſome doubt, with reſpect to Mexico; but not as to any other part of the continent, or any of the iſlands.

Before

Before the discovery of the West Indies, by the Spaniards, in 1492; before the discovery of the East Indies, by the Portuguese navigators, in 1497; and before the discovery of the Brazils, by the same nation, in 1500, abundance of sugar was made in the islands of Sicily, Crete, Rhodes, and Cyprus.

The sugar cane is supposed to have been brought to these islands originally, from India, by the Saracens; and from thence transplanted into some parts of Italy; and to Spain, from Africa, by the Moors.

In Spain, the sugar cane was first planted in Valencia, and afterwards in Granada, and Murcia. Sugar was formerly, in these Southern parts of Spain, produced in great quantity; and some is still made in the two latter provinces.

The celebrated Mr. FRANCIS WILLOUGHBY, who entered Spain from Roussillon, and travelled through great part of it in 1664, says, "at Cullura the wine first begun to be sweet; and three leagues off, at Gandia, in Valencia, the plantations of sugar canes began. Quere, whether the nature of the soil, that was fit to nourish the sugar canes, did not also contribute to the nature of the grapes?

"At Gandia we first found raisins of the sun, as they are called in England; in Spain they call this kind *panſas*, and they ſeem to be the *duracinæ* of the antients. They are all white, round, and have a tougher ſkin than other grapes. They gather them when fully ripe. and dip them in a boiling lixivium of water and aſhes, juſt dipping them in, and taking them out again ; and then dry them upon boards in the ſun, taking them in by night, or in foul weather. The name raiſin comes from *racemus*. Figs are dried juſt as they are gathered, not being dipped in any lixivium.

" I went to Olives, in Valencia alſo, where, and at Gandia, are the engines for ſugar-works ; the beſt are at Olives. By the way we ſaw the ſugar canes growing in ſeveral places. They are planted in low wet grounds, well mucked and dreſſed, divided into beds or hillocks, and furrows. They cut the canes cloſe to the roots in November and December, and, cutting off the ſlender tops, which afford no good juice, keep them under ground till March, and then prick them into theſe hillocks or beds ; out of every *talea*, or cut, ſhoot four, five, or ſix, canes, which will be ripe next December. The knots, or joints of the cane at the bottom, are very cloſe together, ſcarce an inch aſunder ; but upwards the diſtance is more, as the

the cane grows more ſlender. Within is a white pulp, or pith, full of ſap, ſweet as honey. They ſell them at Gandia to eat, and, cutting them in pieces juſt in the middle between two knots, ſuck the pieces at both ends. To make ſugar, after the canes are cleanſed from the tops and leaves, and cut to pieces, they are firſt bruiſed, either with a perpendicular ſtone running round, as apples to make cyder, or olives to make oil; or between two axes ſtrongly capped with iron, horizontally placed, and turned contrary ways; and then preſſed as grapes or olives are. The juice thus preſſed out is boiled in three ſeveral cauldrons, one after another. In the third cauldron it becomes thick and black, and is then put into conical pots, which at the bottom have a little hole ſtopped only with coarſe and foul ſugar. Theſe pots are covered when full with a cake of paſte, made of a kind of earth called the Spaniſh *gritty*, and found near Olives, which is good to take ſpots out of clothes, which cap or cover ſinks as the ſugar ſinks. Theſe conical pots are put into other pots, into which, by the hole at the vertex, the juice drains down through the coarſe ſugar at the bottom. It drains for five or ſix months, in which time the ſugar in the conical pots

 grows

grows hard, and white, all the juice being drunk up by the lute, or run out by the hole in the vertex. The juice is boiled again, ſo long as it is good for any thing; but at laſt it makes only a foul red ſugar, that will never be better. The conical loaves of ſugar, after they are taken out, are ſet to drain over the ſame pots for 14 or 15 days. To make the ſugar more white, they muſt boil it again, but about one-ſixth is loſt every time. A pound of ſugar of 12 ounces is ſold at Olives for three *ſous* and an half; refined, for five or ſix *ſous*. The ſugar juice is ſtrained through ſtrainers of linen, and is put out of one cauldron into another. They take it out of the firſt and ſecond cauldrons ſo ſoon as it begins to boil; but in the third cauldron they let it boil till the ſcum rites, and then take off only the ſcum with the ſcummer, and put it into a long trough, to cool; and, when it is cool, put it into the conical pots. One ſcum riſes after another in the third cauldron. The ſcum, when it is taken off, is white, but turns to a black liquor in the trough. They never refine the ſugar more than three or four times. They uſe for the refining of it whites of eggs, putting in two or three dozen into a cauldron. They uſe but one cauldron for refining. When it is refined, it grows

grows hard and white in nine or ten days. When they refine it, they put a little water into the cauldron, to diſſolve it the better *."

From Valencia, the cultivation of the ſugar cane, and the manufacture of ſugar, were carried in the beginning of the 15th century, by the Spaniards, to the Canary iſlands, and the commerce ariſing from the ſugar there produced was conſiderable: but, prior to this period, the Portugueſe, in 1420, carried the cane, and the manufacture of ſugar, from the iſland of Sicily to Madeira. From theſe origins the cultivation of the ſugar cane, and the art of making ſugar, were extended by different nations of Europeans to the Weſt Indian iſlands, and the Brazils.

Though the Canary iſlands, or *Inſulæ Fortunatæ*, were known to the antients; yet, after the fall of the Roman empire, many centuries elapſed in which all intercourſe, mention, and even knowledge of theſe iſlands, were buried in oblivion; and they remained as ſunk from the world until about the year 1330, when a French veſſel was forced on one of them in a violent gale of wind. After this accident they became known again in Europe.

* RAY's Travels, ed. 1737, vol. I. p. 409.

The conqueſt of theſe iſlands was undertaken by the Spaniards in 1393. The Portugueſe indeed had made ſome ſlight attempts in 1334; but, being repulſed at *Gomero* by the natives, they relinquiſhed the enterprize.

The firſt of theſe iſlands that was conquered was *Lancerata* in 1400; *Fuerventura* was captured in 1405; *Canaria*, in 1483; *Palma*, in 1491; *Teneriff*, in 1495.

The iſland of Madeira is ſuppoſed, like the Canary iſlands, to have been known to the antients; and, like them, to have been loſt in the ſame interval of darkneſs, until the year 1344; when an Engliſh veſſel was driven on this iſland by a ſtorm. But this event was not ſucceeded by any intercourſe with the iſland, and ſeems to have been forgotten, as no notice was taken of it until 1419, when it was again diſcovered by the Portugueſe; who, in the following year, 1420, took poſſeſſion of it. It was then a mere wilderneſs, as its name imports *, and unpeopled. The Portugueſe burnt the woods, and made a ſettlement; and, in the ſame year, planted the ſugar cane there, which they brought from the iſland of Sicily.

* *Maderia.* Nomen factum eſt à Lat. *materia,* quâ tam in vulgatâ Bibliorum verſione quam alibi ſignificatur idem quòd Anglicè *timber*; quia tali materiâ abundabat iſta inſula. Hydii, not. in Peritsol. Itin. p. 113.

From

From the incorrect accounts of the first West Indian discoveries, it is impossible to ascertain in which of the islands the cane was found, and in which it was not. We know it was seen in some of them: but, from modern navigators, we have proofs that it grows spontaneously in all the islands in the South Sea.

It was found in great abundance in all the Society islands, Easter island, and the Sandwich isles; where the Indians are perfectly acquainted with the use of its expressed juice, but have not the knowledge of making sugar.

Some plants of these canes have lately been introduced into the West Indies; and the astonishing increase of sugar, which those brought from Otaheite and planted in Jamaica yield over those of the island, shews, if there be not different species,—that vegetables, as well as animals, may degenerate, and require the impulse of change to incite, or re-animate their vigour.

Thus the breed of cattle, and thus also the improved husbandry in Europe in general, are carried on; grain, seeds, and plants, are removed from place to place, and varied, and cultivated, on physical principles, by philosophers.

In England, the Duke of BEDFORD, and Mr. COKE, have diſtinguiſhed themſelves in this kind of knowledge; and have rendered the moſt eſſential ſervices to their country.

This ſhould be a leſſon to the planter of the ſugar cane, not to continue propagating from the ſame ſtock; or at leaſt to try the effects, where any degeneracy appears, of new plants from another iſland; or from remote parts of the ſame iſland, where the former cannot be obtained.

Whether there be different ſpecies of the ſugar cane, or whether the varieties, with which we have been lately made acquainted, are owing to ſome local cauſes, has not yet been aſcertained.

The French, a few years ſince, introduced into their Weſt Indian iſlands plants from the Eaſt Indies. From their iſlands the cultivation of the Eaſt Indian cane has been carried into ſome of the Engliſh iſlands. Sir JOHN LAFOREY planted them in Antigua, and has proved their preſent ſuperiority over the old canes of the Weſt Indies. He gives the following account of theſe canes:

"One ſort brought from the iſland of Bourbon, reported by the French to be the growth of the coaſt of Malabar.

"Another

"Another ſort from the iſland of Otaheite.

"Another ſort from Batavia.

"The two former are much alike, both in their appearance and growth; but that of Otaheite is ſaid to make the fineſt ſugar. They are much larger than thoſe of our iſlands, the joints of ſome meaſuring eight or nine inches long, and ſix in circumference.

"Their colour, and that of their leaves, alſo differs from ours.

"They are ripe enough to grind, at the age of ten months.

"They appear to ſtand the dry weather better than ours; and are not liable to be attacked by that deſtructive inſect called the *borer*.

"The Batavian canes are a deep purple on the outſide; they grow ſhort-jointed, and ſmall in circumference: but bunch exceedingly, and vegetate ſo quick, that they ſpring up from the plant in one third of the time which thoſe of our iſland do *."

The method of propagating the ſugar cane is by cuttings from the top of it, and we know

* Sir John LAFOREY's remarks on the Eaſt Indian canes, imported into the French Charaibean iſlands, in Mr. EDWARDS's preface to the ſecond edition of his Hiſtory of the Weſt Indies.

of

of no other method; though Mr. BRUCE ſays, in Abyſſinia it is raiſed from the ſeed. Of this fact we have no example; and it is thought that Mr. BRUCE is miſtaken in this matter.

The progreſs of cultivating the cane for the purpoſes of making ſugar, has given riſe to the erroneous ſuppoſition, that the migration of the ſugar cane, under the Europeans, was from Sicily and Spain, to the Madeira and Canary iſlands; and afterwards to the Weſt Indian iſlands, Mexico, Peru, and Brazil: and that it was not an original plant of thoſe iſlands, and countries.

There is, beſides, great difficulty in diſtinguiſhing, in the journals of voyagers, between the hiſtory of the plant and its produce. For, often when ſome particular period is mentioned, when the ſugar cane was firſt carried to countries, the fact is, that ſuch period was the time when the cultivation of the plant, for the purpoſes of making ſugar, was introduced; which before was either entirely neglected, or the uſe of the ſimple juice only known: and frequently mention is made when ſugar was firſt produced in ſome countries, which in reality was the period when the European art of refining it, or ſome improvements in its manufacture, was carried thither.

It

It is certain, that the ſugar cane was found growing in the low, rich lands near the mouth of the Miſſiſippi, when Europeans firſt went to that part of America.

Father HENNEPIN ſays, " from thirty leagues below *Maroa*, down to the ſea, the banks of the Miſſiſippi are full of canes." This was in 1680, when he was there. He was the firſt European who explored the country adjacent to the lower parts of that river.

FRANCIS XIMENES, in his treatiſe on the plants of America, ſays, the ſugar cane grows ſpontaneouſly near the *Rio della Plata*; this is alſo aſſerted by HERNANDES and PISO. This river was diſcovered in 1515, by JOHN DIAS DE SOLIS, a Spaniard; and the country about it conquered by PEDRO DE MENDOZA, in 1535.

JEAN DE LERY, who went in 1556 to the *Rio Janeiro*, in Brazil, ſays, he found every where near that river a great quantity of ſugar canes; and it is certain that they could not have been planted by the Portugueſe, as they were not ſettled in thoſe parts until long afterwards.

JOHN DE LAET ſays, the iſland of St. Vincent produced the ſugar cane ſpontaneouſly. *Lib.* I. *pag.* 27.

LABAT

LABAT ſays, the firſt French ſettlers in St. Chriſtopher, Martinique, and Guadaloupe, found ſugar canes in different parts of thoſe iſlands; which, growing there naturally, were afterwards properly cultivated, and have ſince produced all the Sugar of thoſe iſlands. Vol. II. p. 226.

The iſland of St. Chriſtopher was firſt taken poſſeſſion of by the French and Engliſh, on the ſame day, in the year 1625. The Engliſh made ſugar there in 1643, and the French ſoon after. From this iſland the French ſent a colony to take poſſeſſion of Martinique; and they ſettled there in 1635.

In 1627, the Engliſh ſettled at Barbadoes; and, in 1643, made Sugar there. In 1676 it was in its moſt flouriſhing ſtate, and employed four hundred ſail of veſſels, which were on an average of 150 tons *.

In 1628, the Engliſh ſettled at Nevis.

In 1632, the Engliſh ſettled at Montſerrat; and, in the ſame year, the Dutch ſettled at St. Euſtatia.

In 1635, the French ſettled at Guadaloupe; and, in 1648, made ſugar there.

In 1650, the French ſettled at Granada.

* CHARLES II in 1661, created thirteen Baronets of Barbadoes; each of whom had in the iſland not leſs than a thouſand pounds a-year, and ſome ten thouſand pounds a-year. POSTELTHWAITE.

Jamaica

Jamaica was discovered by COLUMBUS in 1494, in his second voyage; and bestowed on him by Ferdinand and Isabella, as some compensation for the acquisitions he had given to Spain in the West Indies.

His son *James* settled, and planted it in 1509. What improvements it received by the Spaniards, during the time they were in possession of it, are but little known. They continued there however undisturbed until 1596; when Sir ANTHONY SHIRLEY, with a single man of war, took and plundered St. Jago de la Vega; which then consisted of 2000 houses. In the year 1635, this town was again plundered by 500 English from the Leeward islands. In 1656, on the 10th of May, the whole island was reduced, and taken possession of by the forces sent against it by OLIVER CROMWELL; and has since that time belonged to the English.

At this conquest of Jamaica, there were not more than 1500 Spaniards, with about the same number of slaves, in the island. The Spaniards had exterminated all the native Indian inhabitants; not one was seen by the English, out of 60,000 which the Spaniards found there.

The sugar cane was first planted there, by the English, in 1660; and sugar first made in 1664.

1664. But ſome plantations were made there while it was in poſſeſſion of the Spaniards, by ESQUIMEL, a Spaniſh governor, under DIEGO COLUMBUS, ſon of the renowned COLUMBUS; who brought the plants from St. Domingue. There were in Jamaica, on the arrival of the Engliſh, only three ſmall plantations in the iſland; the chief of which was at the *Angels*.

Sir THOMAS MODYFORD, a rich and eminent planter of Barbadoes, was the perſon who firſt planted and cultivated the ſugar cane, for the purpoſe of making ſugar, in Jamaica. This was in 1660. He removed from Barbadoes to Jamaica, and carried with him much agricultural knowlege, to the great advantage of the iſland; which he contributed to improve and benefit, in a very extenſive manner. CHARLES the ſecond appointed him governor of the iſland in 1664; in which ſituation he continued until 1669.

In the iſland of St. Thomas, under the line, on the coaſt of Africa, which was diſcovered by the Portugueſe in 1405, ſugar was made much earlier than in the Weſt Indies.

DAPPER ſays (page 491) that the Portugueſe had ſixty one ſugar works in this iſland, before the Dutch deſtroyed them in the year 1610.

HEYLIN,

HEYLIN, who publiſhed the firſt edition of his Coſmography in 1624, ſays "this iſland is ſo abundant in ſugar canes, and well ſtored with ſugars, that forty ſhips are hence loaded yearly with that one commodity; for making which they have here ſeventy *ingenios*, or ſugar houſes, and in each of them two hundred ſlaves, in ſome three hundred, which belong to the works. Six days in ſeven theſe ſlaves work for their maſters, and the ſeventh for themſelves; which they ſpend in ſewing and planting their ſeeds, fruits, and proviſions. They bring the negroes from the oppoſite continent, with whom the air agrees ſo well, that they attain generally to 110 years; few of the Portugals unto 50. The air is ſo vehemently hot that it ſuiteth not with the conſtitution of the Europeans."

LABAT, Vol. I. pag. 226. is decidedly of opinion, that the ſugar cane is a native plant of the Weſt Indies. But he ſays, that it is to the Portugueſe and Spaniards that Europeans are indebted for the art of making ſugar; who learned the ſecret from the inhabitants of the Eaſt Indies, and returning from thence put it in practice, firſt at the iſland of Madeira and the Canaries, and afterwards in the Brazils, and New Spain, about the end of the year 1580.

That

That the ſugar cane is a native plant of the Weſt Indies there can be no doubt; but in the other remarks, LABAT is miſtaken, as has already appeared; for the Portugueſe had not paſſed the Cape of Good Hope until 1497; long before which time ſugar was made in the Mediterranean Iſlands. Beſides, according to PETER MARTYR, in the year 1518, there were twenty eight ſugar-works in the iſland of Hiſpaniola, eſtabliſhed by the Spaniards. He ſays, "it is a marvellous thing to conſider how all things increaſe and proſper in this iſland. There are now twenty-eight ſugar-preſſes, wherewith great plenty of ſugar is made. The canes or reeds wherein the ſugar groweth are bigger and higher than in any other place; and are as big as a man's wriſt, and higher than the ſtature of a man by the half. This is more wonderful, that whereas in Valencia, in Spain, where a great quantity of Sugar is made yearly, whenſoever they apply themſelves to the great increaſe thereof, yet doth every root bring forth not paſt five, or ſix, or at the moſt ſeven, of thoſe reeds; whereas in Hiſpaniola one root beareth twenty, and oftentimes thirty *." Engliſh edit. 1577, page 172. The original edition was publiſhed in Spain, in 1530.

* This juſtifies the ſuppoſition, that the ſugar cane in the Weſt Indies has degenerated. See page 23.

COLUMBUS,

COLUMBUS, in his firſt voyage in 1492, diſcovered the iſland of Hiſpaniola, or *Saint Domingue*; and ANTONIO HERRARA, in the ſecond book of his ſecond Decad, ſpeaking of the improvements and cultivation carried to that iſland by the Jeronimite friers, ſays, "One AQUILON, an inhabitant of the great plain, carried thither, in the year 1506, ſome ſugar canes from the Canaries, and planted them; the ſame anſwering well, the fathers ordered that every inhabitant, who would erect a ſugar mill, ſhould have five hundred pieces of eight in gold lent him; and, by this contrivance, in a ſhort ſpace of time there came to be forty either Water or Horſe ſugar Mills in the iſland. It is to be obſerved, that formerly ſugar grew only in Valencia, whence it was conveyed to Grenada, thence to the Canaries, and laſtly to the Indies *, which made it more neceſſary to ſend over blacks; and that put the Portugueſe upon carrying many from Guinea. Hiſpaniola proved ſo natural to the blacks, as to have it once ſaid that, unleſs one happened to be hanged, none ever died †."

* This muſt refer only to the manufacturing of ſugar. PISO ſays the ſugar canes were originally found growing wild in the woods in the Canary Iſlands. Lib. 4. Cap. 1.

† HERRARA ſays, the Spaniards firſt imported their negroes from the Portugueſe, who had ſettlements on the coaſt of Africa.

In 1726, the French made in this iſland 33,000 hogſheads of ſugar, of 12 hundred weight each. In 1742, they made 70,666 hogſheads; and, in the ſame year alſo, they made in Martinique, Guadaloupe, and the other leſſer iſles, 51,875 hogſheads.

The whole produce of the Britiſh Weſt Indian Iſlands, imported into Great Britain that year, was 60,950 hogſheads. In 1770, St. Domingue yielded of ſugar, two-thirds brown, 160,000 hogſheads, of 10 hundred weight each.

GONZALES FERDINANDUS OVIEDUS, who lived in Hiſpaniola in 1515, and was governor of the city of *Sancta Maria* in Darien in 1522, ſays, p. 225 of the Summary of his General Hiſtory of the Weſt Indies, "there is ſuch abundance of ſugar in Mexico, that certain Spaniſh ſhips are yearly freighted therewith, and bring the ſame unto Seville, in Spain; from whence it is carried to all parts of Chriſtendom."

As Mexico was not entirely conquered by the Spaniards until 1521, I think it is clear that the ſugar cane muſt have been cultivated, and ſugar made in Mexico, before the Spaniards went thither.

PETER

PETER CIEZA, who travelled from the year 1533 to 1550, in Peru, and other parts of South America, ſays, cap. 64, p. 167, "In ſeveral parts of the vales, near the city of St. Michael, there are large fields of ſugar canes, whereof ſugar is made in ſeveral towns and preſerves."

He mentions this among other articles of the agriculture of the Indians, before the Spaniards went among them; for, though VASCO NUNEZ DE BALBOA croſſed to the South Sea, and ſettled at Panama in 1513, yet the Spaniards were never in any part of Peru before the year 1525; and then PIZARRO, with a few adventurers, only landed, and made ſome diſcoveries, but returned to Spain in 1528, for authority to undertake the conqueſt of Peru; which was not begun in South America until 1530, and completed in 1532, by the murder of the laſt Inca, Atabalipa; or, as the Spaniards write the name, *Atahuallpa:* yet Spain was not in peaceable poſſeſſion of Peru before 1554.

This immenſe ſcene of blood was not cloſed by the Spaniards, without many tragical events among themſelves. ALMAGRO, the conqueror of Chili, was ſtrangled before Cuſco by HERNAND PIZARRO in 1538; and FRANCIS PIZARRO,

 the

the conqueror of Peru, was aſſaſſinated at Lima in 1541, by the partizans of ALMAGRO.

CIEZA mentions alſo the manner in which the Indians carry water in trenches, from the rivers deſcending from the mountains, through the fields in the plains; to ſupply the defect of rain in thoſe countries.

This part of Peru was then inhabited entirely by Indians; for, though *St. Michael* was the firſt city built by the Spaniards in Peru, it was not founded until 1541, by PIZARRO, before the capture of *Atabalipa*; and, conſequently, before the wars were ended, or that the Spaniards had turned their thoughts to agriculture. Wherefore, it is probable that the art of making ſugar was known to the Peruvian Indians alſo, before the Spaniards went among them.

It is certain that GARCILASSO DE LA VEGA, who was a native of Peru, and left that country and went to Spain in the year 1560, ſays, in his Commentaries, lib. IX. cap. 28, part 1, that "antiently there were no ſugar canes in Peru, though now, by the induſtry of the Spaniards, and the fertility of the ſoil, they are increaſed to a loathſome plenty; that, whereas formerly they were highly eſteemed, and are now become of no value or eſtimation."

"The

" The firſt Sugar Works in Peru were made in *Huanca*, by the contrivance of a gentleman with whom I was well acquainted. A ſervant of his, who was a ſubtile and ingenious perſon, obſerving the great quantities of ſugar which were imported from Mexico, by reaſon of which the ſugar of Peru would not ſell to any account, adviſed his maſter to ſend one ſhip's lading of his ſugar to Mexico; that they, ſeeing thereby the plenty of that commodity in Peru, might forbear to ſend any more thither. The project ſucceeded according to expectation; and now ſugar works are erected in many places in that country "

JOSEPH ACOSTA, who was in South America about the year 1580, ſays, in his Natural and Moral Hiſtory of the Indies, lib. IV. cap. 32, " that they not only uſe a great deal of ſugar in the Indies, but alſo carry much into Spain; for, the canes grow exceedingly well in many parts of the Indies. They have built their engines in the iſlands, in Mexico, in Peru, and in other parts; which yieldeth the Spaniards a very great revenue."

" It was told me, that the engine for making ſugar in *Naſca*, in Peru, was worth yearly above thirty thouſand pieces of revenue. That of *Chicama*, joining to *Truxillo*, in the ſame country, was likewiſe of great revenue, and thoſe of New Spain are of no leſs: and it is ſtrange to ſee what ſtore they conſume at the Indies. They brought from the iſland of *Saint Domingue*, in the fleet wherein I came, 898 cheſts of ſugar, which being, as I did ſee, ſhipped at *Porto Rico*, every cheſt, in my opinion, weighed eight *arobes*, every *arobes* we ghing five and twenty pounds, which are two hundred weight of ſugar. This is the chief revenue of theſe iſlands, ſo much are men given to ſweet things."

THOMAS GAGE, who went to New Spain in 1625, ſays (p. 236), in the voyage the Spaniſh fleet, in which he was, touched at the iſland of *Guadaloupe*; "where the Indians with great joy yearly expect the Spaniſh fleets; and by the moons reckon the months, and thereby gueſs at their coming; and ſome prepare ſugar canes, others plantains, others turtles, ſome one proviſion, ſome another, to barter with the Spaniards for their ſmall haberdaſhery, iron, knives, and ſuch things which may help them in their wars, which commonly they make againſt ſome other iſlands."

This was ten years before any Europeans had ſettled there; and where no ſugar was made until 1648, by the French, who then poſſeſſed

poſſeſſed it. The ſugar cane, conſequently, was the natural production of that Iſland.

GAGE ſays, cap. 15, "two or three leagues from the Indian town of *Chiapa* there are (in 1626) two Ingenios or Farms of ſugar, one belonging to the cloiſter of the Dominicans of the Spaniſh city of *Chiapa*, which is twelve leagues from this town, the other to the cloiſter of this town, which contain near two hundred Black-Moors, beſides many Indians, who are employed in that conſtant work of making ſugar for all the country."

He alſo remarks, in the ſame chapter, that ſugar was an article of commerce, and ſent from *Chiapa* down the river *Tabaſco*, to be tranſported to the Havannah. The towns of *Chiapa* are in the province of *Chiapa*, which joins to *Guatimala*.

The Portugueſe firſt eſtabliſhed Sugar Works in the Brazils, in 1580. They had no ſettlement of conſequence there before 1549. The Dutch, after the truce between Spain and Holland in 1562, began their expeditions to the Brazils; and in 1637 they ſent Count MAURICE thither. In 1641, when the treaty of peace was concluded between the Dutch and Portugueſe, the former were in number 20,000, and had acquired ſeven of the fourteen captain-

 ſhips

ſhips of Brazil. They had 60,000 negroes there, and made 25,000 cheſts of ſugar. But, in 1655, they were diſpoſſeſſed of their territories, and ceded them by treaty, in 1661, to the Portugueſe; being reduced in number, by wars and other diſaſters, to only ſix or ſeven hundred perſons. It was theſe Dutch fugitives, driven from the Brazils in 1655, that carried the art of planting the cane, and making ſugar in a proper manner, to the Weſt Indian Iſlands.

I have before obſerved, that the iſland of Barbadoes was firſt ſettled by the Engliſh in 1627, and ſugar made there in 1643. I ſhall now add ſome particulars from LIGON, which will illuſtrate the ſubject in a very ſatisfactory manner.

He ſays, in his Hiſtory of Barbadoes, p. 85, "At the time we landed on this iſland, which was in the beginning of September, 1647, we were informed, partly by thoſe planters we found there, and partly by our own obſervations, that the great work of ſugar-making was but newly practiſed by the inhabitants there. Some of the moſt induſtrious men, having gotten plants from *Fernambrock*, a place in Brazil, and made trial of them at the Barbadoes, and finding them to grow, they planted

planted more and more, as they grew and multiplied on the place, till they had ſuch a conſiderable number as they were worth the while to ſet up a very ſmall Ingenio, and ſo make trial what ſugar could be made on that ſoil. But the ſecrets of the work being not well underſtood, the ſugars they made were very inconſiderable, and little worth, for two or three years. But they, finding their errors by their daily practice, began a little to mend; and, by new directions from Brazil, ſometimes by ſtrangers, and now and then by their own people, who were content ſometimes to make a voyage thither, to improve their knowledge in a thing they ſo much deſired. Being now much better able to make their queries, of the ſecrets of that myſtery, by how much their often-failings had put them to often-ſtops and nonpluſſes in the work. And ſo returning with more plants, and better knowlege, they went on upon freſh hopes, but ſtill ſhort of what they ſhould be more ſkilful in; for, at our firſt arrival, we found them ignorant in three main points that much conduced to the work; *viz.* the manner of planting; the time of gathering; and the right placing their coppers in their furnaces; as alſo the true way of covering their rollers with plates or bars of iron.

iron. At the time of our arrival there we found many ſugar works ſet up, and at work: but yet the ſugars they made were but bare Muſcovadoes; and few of them merchantable commodities; ſo moiſt, and full of molaſſes, and ſo ill cured, as they were hardly worth bringing home to England. But about the time I left the iſland, which was in 1650, they were much bettered; for then they had ſkill to know when the canes were ripe, which was not till they were fifteen months old; and before they gathered them at twelve, which was a main diſadvantage to the making good ſugar; for, the liquor wanting of the ſweetneſs it ought to have, cauſed the ſugars to be lean, and unfit to keep. Beſides, they had grown greater proficients both in boiling and curing them, and had learnt the knowlege of making them white, ſuch as you call lump-ſugars here in England; but not ſo excellent as thoſe they make in Brazil; nor is there any likelihood they can ever make ſuch; the land there being better, and lying in a continent, muſt needs have conſtanter and ſteadier weather, and the air much drier and purer than it can be in ſo ſmall an iſland as that of Barbadoes."

HISTORY

HISTORY

OF

SUGAR.

SUGAR was firſt brought into Europe from Arabia and the Eaſt. What kind or ſpecies of ſugar this was, or whether any of the various preparations of it now in uſe, has been a ſubject of much controverſy in antiquarian literature.

The profoundedly learned SALMASIUS (SAUMAISE, his proper name), who went to reſide at Leyden in 1632, aſſerts, that what authors denominate the *ſacar mambu* of the Indians, was the σακχαρον, or ſugar, of the ancients.

By the term ancients, in this treatiſe, the Greeks and Romans of the earlier periods are not meant. To them the word ſugar was unknown.

He

He ſays,—*Exercitationes noſtræ docent illud σακχαρον eſſe quod hoc tempore vocatur apud Indos Sacar-Mambu ; quod in arundine Indica arboreæ ac vaſtæ proceritatis ſponte creſcit.* De Saccharo Commentarius.

He alſo ſays, this *ſàcar-mambu* of the Indians was the *tabaxir* of the Arabians ; but that the Arabians were ignorant how it was produced, as were the ancient Greeks of the *generatio Mellis Calamini, ſive σακχαρου* ; who thought it was the dew, which, falling on the Indian canes, concreted : and that it was a kind of manna.

The Arabians, he obſerves, ſuppoſed the *tabaxir* to be the aſhes of the cane ; and certainly, he ſays, this ſpecies of ſugar, when concreted and coagulated, is like aſhes ; but, when iſſuing from the joints of the cane, it is white like ſtarch. The antients remark alſo, that their ſugar was brittle between the teeth ; therefore many of them call it *Indian ſalt* ; whereas our ſugar, he ſays, melts in the mouth, and is not brittle *.

He contends, that the Arabians were in an error reſpecting their *tabaxir* ; and that it was not the aſhes of the cane, but the *ſacar-mambu*

* *Exercitationes Plinianæ.*

of

of the Indians, and the real *μελι καλαμινον* of the Greeks. He ſays the antients gave it the appellation of ſugar, which the Arabians did not; becauſe they believed it to be aſhes, and not a ſpecies of ſugar which was called by them *zuchar*.

He ſays the cane, from which the fictitious ſugar now in uſe is made, is a ſmall plant; but that in the Indies, which yields the *ſacar-mambu* of the Indians, the *tabaxir* of the Arabians, or native ſugar of the antients, is a large tree; and that this ſpecies of ſugar is the concreted exudation from the tree, found about the joints.

SALMASIUS at length attempts, as a farther corroboration of his opinion, to ſhew, that the virtues attributed by the Arabians to the *tabaxir*, coincide with thoſe which the Greeks aſcribed to their *σακχαρον*.

In theſe conjectures, I believe, it will appear that the moſt learned SALMASIUS is miſtaken; and that the *tabaxir*, or, as it has been variouſly rendered by tranſlators, *thabaſir*, *tarathit*, *ſataiſcir*, *tabaſis*, *tabaſir*, *and ſabaſcir*, of RHASIS, AVICENNA, SERAPION, and AVERROES, was neither the *ſacar-mambu* of the Indians, nor the *σακχαρον* of the antients.

Let

Let us examine what may be collected from the Arabians themſelves, concerning their *tabaxir.*

RHASES *(anno* 930*)* ſays,—

Tarathit, id eſt Spodium, frigida eſt & ſicca, quæ & ventrem ſtringit, & ſanguinem exire prohibet. Spodium frigidum eſt & ſiccum, quod febribus acutis, ac ſiti, & nimio ventris fluxui, & vomitui, confert: puſtulis quoque quæ in ore & lingua naſcuntur, atque tremori cordis, auxiliatur. De Simplicibus, cap. 36.

AVICENNA *(anno* 1040*)* ſays,—*Thabaſir* (the tranſlator calls it *Spodium) quid eſt? Cannarum aduſtæ; dicitur enim quod ipſæ aduruntur propter fricationem ſuarum extremitatum, quum ventus eas perflat. Frigidum eſt in ſecundo, & ſiccum in tertio. In ipſo eſt ſtipticitas, & præparatio & parum reſolutionis, & ejus infrigidatio eſt plurima, & ejus reſolutio eſt propter amaritudinem paucam in ipſo. Ex reſolutione igitur ejus, & ſtipticitate, fit exſiccatio fortis, & eſt compoſitarum virtutum ſicut roſa. Confert aphthis, & melancholiæ provenienti ſolitudine. Spodium (Tabaxir) confert apoſtematibus oculi calidis, confortat cor, et confert tremori ejus calido, & ſyncopi factæ ex effuſione choleræ ad ſtomachum, & bibitum, & linitum, & confert melancholiæ ex ſolicitudine, & timori*

timori de præteritis, & terrori de futuris. Confert tuſſi (ſiti) & inflammationi ſtomachi, & debilitati ejus, & prohibet effuſionem choleræ ad ipſum, & confert conturbationi. Prohibet ſolutionem cholericam. Confert febribus acutis. Lib. II. tract. 2. cap. 616. Ed. Venetiis, 1595.

SERAPION *(anno* 1070*)* ſays, adducing his authorities,—

Sataiſcir, vel Reſcius, id eſt Spodium.

BEDIGORES,—*Proprietatis ſpodii eſt, quod confert caliditati choleræ.*

RHASES, *ex verbo* GALENI,—*In ſpodio eſt reſolutio, & prohibitio, & repercuſſio, & infrigidatio, ſed infrigidatio ejus eſt fortior, & in ſapore ejus eſt amaritudo, & ſtipticitas, & propter hoc deſiccat. Et jam eſt declaratum, quod in ſpodio eſt virtus compoſita, ſicut roſa, & non eſt in ſpodio tantum ſtipticitas, quantum in roſa.*

DIOSCORIDES,—*Spodium confert apoſtematibus calidis oculorum.*

MESEAH,—*Spodium eſt frigidum in tertio gradu, ſiccum in ſecundo, confert inflationi choleræ, & fortificat ſtomachum, et confert ulceribus oris.*

MESARUGIE,—*Eſt bonum choleræ, & ſyncopi, et bother (puſtulis) factis in ore puerorum.*

RHASES,—

RHASES,—*Spodium eſt frigidum et ſiccum in tertio gradu, ſtringit ventrem, et confert ulceribus oris, et inflationi choleræ, et fortificat ſtomachum, et confert ſyncopi, et cardiacæ calidæ quando datur in potu ex eo, et confert bother (puſtulis) frigidis in ore infantium.* De Temperamentis, Simplicium, cap. 332.

AVERROES, (*anno* 1198) ſays,

Tabaiſis, id eſt ſpodium, carbo eſt nodorum arundinum aduſtarum Indiæ: frigidum eſt & ſiccum in tertio gradu, et ejus proprietas eſt removere caliditatem et inflammationem choleræ, et confortat ſtomachum, et confert cardiacæ calidæ. De Simplicibus, cap. 56.

Now it is evident, from the teſtimony of the preceding authors, that the Arabians aſcribed no property whatever to their *tabaxir*, which is any way applicable to ſugar. The great feature of its character, *ſweetneſs*, is not once mentioned.

The tranſlators, as their originals before them, had conſidered the *tabaxir* to be the aſhes of the Indian canes; or of their joints, or roots: and being of a greyiſh colour, like *ſpodium*, *(pompholix, tutty, putty)* rendered the word *tabaxir*, by that appellation, from σποδος, aſhes. But as it was given internally, it certainly

tainly could not be the σποδος of the Greeks; which was the ſordes, or recrement of melting braſs: and never employed by them but for external purpoſes.

Salmasius, whoſe great erudition and extenſive knowledge have been the admiration of the learned in every country, never ſelected a ſubject for his animadverſions, with which he appears to have been ſo little acquainted as the preſent. He conceals, beneath a dazzling diſplay of learning, the imperfect knowledge he had of the hiſtory of ſugar: taken chiefly from uninformed travellers, and particularly from Garcias ab *Orta*, in reſpect to the *tabaxir.*

Garcias, who was a Portugueſe phyſician, and lived at Goa in the Eaſt Indies, in 1563, ſays "the *tabaxir* of the Arabians, rendered *ſpodium* by their interpreters, is not the ſpodium of the Greeks: which is a metallic preparation, and never given internally. They differ as much as black from white; and that the ſpodium of the Greeks is the *tutty* of the Arabians."

He ſays that "*tabaxir* is a Perſian word, which Avicenna and other Arabian writers took from the Perſian language; and that it implies, *lactens humor, aut ſuccus liquorve alicubi concretus:* by which name this medicine is known to the Arabians and Turks."

He ſays "the Indians call it *ſacar-mambu*, that is, the ſugar of the *mambu*; becauſe the Indian canes, or trees, the branches of which produce it, are ſo called. But that they now call it *tabaxir* alſo; as by that name it is ſent for from Arabia, Perſia, and Turkey, and is imported, as an article of commerce, into thoſe countries from India."

He ſays "the *tabaxir* is a very dear medicine in Arabia, and ſells for its weight in ſilver."

The tree which produces it, he ſays, "is ſometimes as large as a poplar tree; ſometimes ſmaller; the branches generally grow erect (unleſs when bent for bowers and ſhady walks, cuſtomary among the Indians), with knots, the length of the hand aſunder; with a leaf reſembling the Olive leaf, but longer. Between each of the joints, a ſweetiſh liquor is generated, thick like ſtarch, and like it in whiteneſs; ſometimes much, but ſometimes very little. All the canes, or branches, do not contain this liquor, but only thoſe which grow in Biſnager, Batecala, and part of the province of Malabar."

This

This liquor when concreted is ſometimes found blackiſh, or of a grey colour, but it is not the worſe on that account; becauſe it ariſes from too great humidity, or that it has been retained too long in the wood, which makes it of this colour; but not from the burning of the tree, as ſome have ſuppoſed."

He then recites the opinion of RHASES, reſpecting the virtues of the *tabaxir*, and obſerves that in the latin verſion of SERAPION, it has been corruptly rendered *ſataiſcir*. He ſays "it is evident from what is ſtated, that AVICENNA was miſtaken in ſuppoſing the *tabaxir* to be the aſhes of the roots of the canes."

He ſays alſo, as a further proof of the *tabaxir* and *ſpodium* having been erroneouſly confounded together, "that *ſpodium* was not uſed internally by the Greeks; and that, by the teſtimony of the Indian, Arabian, Perſian, and Turkiſh phyſicians, the *tabaxir* is uſed not only in external, but in internal inflammations; and alſo in bilious fevers and dyſenteries." *Hiſtoria Aromatum*, *lib.* I. *cap.* 12.

PISO, a Dutch phyſician, who lived in the Braſils in the beginning of the laſt century, ſays, "in Egypt the *ſacar* of the Arabians, from whence our word ſugar is derived, is produced from a low and little plant, coagulated by the heat of the ſun ; but, in the Eaſt Indies, from the *mambu reed tree*, (he then refers to GARCIAS, whom he little more than copies in the whole article,) which is full of joints, and in ſize as large as the poplar tree. The *ſacar-mambu*, which the Arabians call *tabaxir*, iſſues from this tree, a viſcid whitiſh liquor, according to RHAZES, AVICENNA, and SERAPION." *Hiſt. Nat. & Med. lib.* IV. *cap.* 1.

He ſays, in another place, that " there are in the uncultivated regions of the Indies two ſpecies of canes, called *Mambu* ; or, as the Portugueſe have corrupted the word into, *Bambu*. One ſort is ſmall and full of pith ; and the other large, and more hollow : for which reaſon they have been called by writers ſometimes canes, and ſometimes trees."

He then gives an account, not much deviating from GARCIAS, concerning the uſes, and other particulars, of the *Bambu* cane ; obſerving, " that there are ſome ſo large, that the Indians make canoes of them, capable of carrying two people."

He ſays, " the full-grown *Mambu* canes have a ſoft, ſpongy, liquid, medullary ſubſtance, which

which the common people ſuck with avidity, on account of its grateful taſte."

"When theſe canes are large and old, the liquor which they contain changes in colour, taſte, and efficacy, and gradually protudes through the cane, between the joints, and is coagulated by the heat of the ſun, and hardens like white *pummice* ſtone, and ſoon loſes its native agreeableneſs of flavour, and acquires a taſte ſomething like burnt ivory, and is called by the Indians *ſacar-mambu.* The lighter, whiter, and ſmoother it is, the more it is eſteemed; and the more cineritious it is in colour and unequal in figure, the worſe."

"It is held in eſtimation by the Indian, Arabian, Mooriſh, Perſian, and Turkiſh phyſicians, for external and internal heats and inflammations, and bilious dyſenteries; and the Indians uſe it in ſtranguries, gonorrhœas, and hæmorrhages."

"The word *tabaxir* is taken from the Perſian language, and ſignifies *lac lapideſcens*, which ſome credulous Arabians and Turks thought to be the aſhes of canes, burnt by the friction produced by the wind blowing them together. This error has been propagated by the Latin interpreters of the Arabians, rendering *tabaxir*, *ſpodium*; becauſe in taſte and appearance it

 ſomewhat

ſomewhat reſembles burnt ivory or hartſhorn. But, as GARCIAS obſerves, *ſpodium*, or *tutty*, is uſed only externally in the compoſitions of the Greeks; and *ſacar-mambu*, or *tabaxir*, is generally uſed in the compoſitions of the Arabians, for internal purpoſes."

"The Indians have uſed the word *Sacar* in their language for this concreted juice, not on account of any ſweetneſs in it, for many centuries. In after-times, when the art of making ſugar from the expreſſed juice of the ſugar-cane was known, that factitious ſubſtance received the appellation of *ſaccharum*, or ſugar: probably deriving its etymology from the *ſacar* of the Indians." *Mantiſſ. Aromat. cap.* 10.

He makes many other remarks, chiefly copied from GARCIAS and SALMASIUS.

LINSCHOTON ſays, "there are over all India many ſugar canes in all places, and in great numbers, but not much eſteemed of: all along the coaſt of Malabar there are many thick reeds, eſpecially on the coaſt of Coromandel, which reeds by the Indians are called *mambu*, and by the Portugueſe *bambu*; theſe mambu's have a certain matter within them, which is, as it were, the pith of it, ſuch as quills have within them, which men take out when they make

make their pens to write. The Indians call it *ſacar-mambu*, which is as much as to ſay, ſugar of *mambu*, and is a very medicinable thing much eſteemed, and much ſought for by the Arabians, Perſians, and Moors: they call it *tabaxir*. *Cap.* 4. *anno* 1583.

I think it is evident, from the authors above cited, that, ſuppoſing the *ſacar-mambu* of the Indians were the *tabaxir* of the Arabians, it is impoſſible it could be the *ſaccharum* of the ancients.

It is alſo unneceſſary to contend that the *ſacar-mambu* of the Indians was not the *tabaxir* of the Arabians; for it appears to me that neither GARCIAS, nor his follower PISO, were poſitive, from their own knowledge, what the *ſacar-mambu* is.

It is certain that the *ſacar-mambu* is not ſweet, according to their account, and conſequently cannot have any relation to ſugar: and if it be the exuded gummous juice of the *mambu*, or, as we call it, the *bambu-cane*, it could not be ſweet, for that tree contains no ſaccharine juice. How then could this be the ſugar of the ancients?

The Arabians had their *tabaxir* from India. Their account of it is fabulous. Yet they all agree that it was the ashes of the Indian cane: and whether it was a kind of pot-ash, or any other saline preparation, from vegetable exci-neration, we cannot determine from any chemical or medical facts they have left us on the subject. Certain it is, there is no *sweetness* attributed to it, and consequently it could not be sugar; and, as it was given internally, whatever resemblance it might have to *spodium*, it has no right to that interpretation; as the *spodium* of the Greeks, as already observed, was a metallic preparation, and never used internally.

The Arabian medical writers were chiefly compilers and copiers from the Greeks; and seem to have known but little, even of their own country. Their account of *manna* is as fabulous as that of their *tabaxir*, and has given rise to as many speculations. They supposed it was a dew, attracted by certain trees, plants, and stones, and there concreted.

AVICENNA denominates manna, a species of sugar, *zuccarum albusar*; which, he says, falls on the plant *albusar*, or *albossar*, and is there collected in lumps, like salt.

Zuccarum albusar quid est? Manna; cadens super albusar, et est sicut frusta salis. Lib. II. tract. II. cap. 756.

SERAPION,

SERAPION, *cap.* 45. *de Temperamentis Simplicium*, ſpeaking of *men*, or *manna*, ſays, from RHASES, when it firſt falls on the leaves of the trees, it is like honey, but green, which, by remaining there for ſome time, becomes white. He ſays alſo, from MESCHA, that its qualities depend on the nature of the trees on which it falls. He has another ſpecies of manna, *cap.* 41. which he calls *tereniabin*,—*mel roris*, and which he ſays, from EBENAMREZ, falls on trees with thorns, in the Eaſt.

The Arabian writers were all unacquainted with the real nature of manna, in ſuppoſing it to be dew, inſtead of the inſpiſſated juice of trees.

RHAZES ſays, *cap.* 20. *de Simplicibus*,—*teroniabin* is hot, purges the bowels, and aſſuages the throat.

Indeed, AVERROES himſelf, in ſome meaſure, accounts for their being unacquainted with it, by ſaying, it was not the produce of their own country.—

Terregebim, id eſt manna, provenit à partibus ſuperioribus Syriæ, vel Indiæ. cap. 55. Simplicia.

However, a different inference may be drawn from AVICENNA, who ſays, there are two ſorts of manna, and both the produce of Arabia. The

The white ſort from *Iamen*, or *Yemen*; and the dark ſort from *Agizium*, or *Hagiazi*. The former of theſe places is in Arabia Felix, and the latter in Arabia Deſerta;—

Aliud eſt Iamenum, album; et aliud eſt Agizium, ad nigridinem declinans.

Lib. II. tract. II. cap. 756.

AVICENNA mentions a ſugar, which is found on canes, like ſalt:—

Illud ſaccharum, quod ſuper àrundinem invenitur, ſicut ſal. De Zuccaro, lib. II. tract. 2. cap. 755.

SALMASIUS, believing in this error, that ſugar was actually found ready made, aſſerts,—

De hoc ipſo priſcorum ſaccharo, ſive tabaxir, accepi debet; cui nomen etiam propterea αλος Ινδικου *veteres impoſuerunt.* De Canteo, cap. 79.

"This is the ſugar of the ancients, to which they alſo gave the name of *Indian Salt*; it is alſo the *tabaxir* of the Arabians."

I have already ſhewn that this was not ſugar, or any ſaccharine ſubſtance.

I have not given all the Latin verſions of the Arabian writers in Engliſh, for reaſons obvious to the learned.

What ſeems to have ſtrengthened SALMASIUS in this error is, that the ſugar deſcribed by the ancients

ancients does not correſpond with any ſpecies of ſugar now in uſe. His own words are,—

Fallitur itaque mirum in modum ſi quis μελι καλαμινον, aut αλας Ινδικον, aut σακχαρον antiquum idem putat cum noſtro ſaccharo. De Saccharo Comment.

It may now be proper to ſee what the ancients have left on record relative to our ſubject, in order to aſcertain what evidence may be obtained from their writings, by which we may decide on the ſuppoſitions and opinions which have been advanced; and I apprehend it will appear, that the ſugar known to the ancients was neither the *ſaccar-mambu* of the Indians, nor the *tabaxir* of the Arabians, nor, as many have imagined, *manna.*

Dioscorides *(anno* 64), who is the firſt writer which mentions the word σακχαρον, or ſugar, in his chapter περι Σακχαρου Μελιτος, demonſtrates clearly that he was acquainted with ſome ſpecies of ſugar, made from the ſugar cane; though it plainly appears that he was ignorant of the nature of its preparation.—

Καλειται δε τι και σακχαρον ειδος ον μελιτος, εν Ινδια πεπηγοτος και τη ευδαιμονι Αραβια· ευρισκομενον

ευρισκομενον επι των καλαμων, ομοιον τη συστασει αλισι, και θραυομενον υπο τοις οδουσι καθαπερ οι αλες.

" There is a ſort of concreted honey, which is called ſugar, found upon canes, in India and Arabia Felix: it is in conſiſtence like ſalt, and it is brittle between the teeth like ſalt."

Pliny ſays,—

Saccaron & Arabia fert, ſed laudatius India. Eſt autem mel in harundinibus collectum, gummium modo, candidum, dentibus fragile; ampliſſimum nucis avellanæ magnitudine: ad medicinæ tantum uſum. Hiſt. Nat. lib. XII. cap. 8.

" Sugar is brought from Arabia, but the beſt ſort from India. It is honey collected from canes, like a gum, white, and brittle between the teeth; the largeſt is of the ſize of an hazle nut: it is uſed in medicine only."

Arrian (*anno* 123), *in Periplo maris Erythræi*, ſays, there is a nation bordering on the Red Sea, who drink, *μελι το καλαμινον, το λεγομενον σακχαρι*;—" honey of the reed, called ſugar."

Galen

Galen (*anno* 164), in his 7th book of the temperaments and faculties of ſimple medicines, *περι Μελιτος*, ſays,—

Και το σακχαρ δε καλουμενον οπερ εξ Ινδιας τε και της ευδαιμονος Αραβιας κομιζεται περι πηγνυται μεν, ως φασι, καλαμοις, εστι δε τι και αυτο μελιτος ειδος· ηττον μεν ουν εστιν, η το παρ ημιν γλυκυ.

"Sugar, as they call it, which is brought from India and Arabia Felix, concretes, as they ſay, about the canes, and is a ſpecies of honey: it is leſs ſweet than our honey."

Paulus Æginetа (*anno* 670), the laſt of the Greek writers on medicine, *lib.* II. *cap.* 54. ſays, from Archigenes, who lived *anno* 117,—

Αλς ο Ινδικος, χροια μεν και συστασει, ομοιος τῷ κοινῷ αλι, γευσει δε μελιτωδης.

"The *Indian ſalt*, in colour and form like common ſalt, but in taſte and ſweetneſs like honey."

In *lib.* VII. *cap.* 3, he ſays, "Honey is of an heating and drying nature in the ſecond degree, and is abundantly cleanſing. Boiled, it is leſs lefs acrid and deterfive, and opens the bowels, but is more nutritious: but the bitter honey, fuch as comes from Sardonia, has the mixed property of being earthy and hot. The *other fugar*, which is brought from Arabia Felix, is lefs fweet than that which we have: but it has equal virtues, and is neither hurtful to the ftomach, nor excites thirft like our honey."

It is true that DIOSCORIDES, PLINY, GALEN, and P. ÆGINETA, all mention that fugar came from Arabia as well as from India; but it is certain that the fugar defcribed by them to be "white like falt, and brittle between the teeth, and fweet like honey," was brought from India into Arabia; and was not the produce of Arabia; and this is proved by what follows.

AVICENNA recommends, from ARCHIGENES, as quoted by P. ÆGINETA, when the tongue is dry and parched in fevers, to cleanfe it with oil of almonds and white fugar; and that the fick fhould have in his mouth a lump of "the falt that is brought from India; which in colour is like falt, and in fweetnefs like honey."—

"*Sal, qui afportatur de India, & in colore falis, & dulcidine mellis.*" De Afperitate Linguæ, lib. IV. fen. 1. tr. 2. cap. 22.

Here

Here we have, I think, decidedly the ſugar of the ancients.

This can be no other preparation than that we now call white SUGAR-CANDY; which I conſider as the real μελι καλαμινον: αλς Ινδικος:—σακχαρον *antiquorum*.

It is evident AVICENNA erroneouſly ſuppoſed this ſaccharine preparation as a natural, and not as an artificial production; when, ſpeaking of the different ſorts, or rather coloured ſugars, he compares it in appearance to ſalt; and ſays it is found on canes, in the paſſage before mentioned.

In different parts of this treatiſe, I have ſelected from the Arabians every thing they have ſaid pertaining to the ſubject; but there is ſuch a want of diſcrimination among the Arabian writers, which their editors, tranſlators, and commentators, have further perplexed with various texts, interpretations, and conjectures, that it is impoſſible to know exactly the preciſe diſtinctions, intended by the original authors, in their different appellations of *honey*, *manna*, and *ſugar*.

However, the ſugar cane is unqueſtionably a native plant of ſome parts of Arabia; and, though the art of evaporating its juice for the purpoſe of making a common, coarſe, or muſ-

covado

covado ſugar, was known long before AVICENNA's time; yet I cannot ſuppoſe, a thouſand years prior to his time, that the ſugar of the ancients, being ſugar-candy, was made in Arabia; eſpecially as AVICENNA himſelf, if we admit the *ſalt* he mentions to be the ſame, ſays it was brought to Arabia from India.

Yet PLINY is very particular, in obſerving that the Indian ſugar was ſuperior in quality to the Arabian; which ſhews, that ſome of the ſugar known to the Romans in his time, muſt have been brought from Arabia, if not manufactured there.

Beſides, we know that there is no ſuch thing as ſugar found on canes; and, ſo far from the juice of the cane iſſuing from the plant, and concreting like gummous or vegetable rezinous juices, the plant decays on being wounded; and, without being wounded, the juice never eſcapes from its ſtem.

Every kind of ſugar whatever is made by art. Native ſugar never exiſted. Ignorant people, even at this day, in our own part of the world, imagine that ſugar is found, like pith, in the hollow of the canes; in the ſtate in which it is brought to Europe.

The cryſtalline appearance of ſugar-candy, and its fragility between the teeth, might naturally

turally lead the ancient writers to give it the appellation of *ſalt*; eſpecially as the ſalt uſed by them was rock, or foſſile ſalt, in form and pieces ſimilar to ſugar-candy: and, from its ſweetneſs, that of *honey* of the *reed*; as honey was their ſtandard of ſweetneſs.

It was alſo very natural, for people who knew nothing of the proceſs of making ſugar, that they ſhould conſider it, being a vegetable production, as a gum; and, like other gums, to be the exudations of ſome plant, or tree, concreted by the heat of the ſun.

There can be no doubt but that the ſugar of the ancients, and that ſpecies of ſugar deſcribed by the Arabians as reſembling ſalt, with the ſweetneſs of honey, were the ſame article; and as in the writing of the ancients there is only one ſort of ſugar mentioned, and though that ſugar is ſaid by ſome of them to have been brought from Arabia, as well as from India, yet the Arabians themſelves mention it as brought from India only; and there is every reaſon to believe, at that period, the art of chryſtallizing the juice of canes was underſtood only in India.

Indeed, ſugar muſt have been better known in Greece and in Italy, from their contiguity to Arabia, had it then been manufactured in that country. Befides, there is no mention among the antients of any kind of fweet canes or reeds, but what were particularly faid to have grown in India.

As it is certain that fugar was brought from India at the time when mention was firft made of it, it is proper to enquire whether it was manufactured in India only ; and what fort of fugar was made in India in thofe times ; or at leaft to draw the beft inference we can from what we know of the hiftory of the commerce of fugar, and the manufacture of it in the Eaft Indies, at this time.

There have ever been, fince our knowledge of the Eaft, two forts of fugar made there ; raw or mufcovado fugar, and fugar-candy ; the firft ufed only for culinary purpofes, and the latter for every other purpofe of diet, luxury, and exportation.

The art of refining fugar, and making what is called loaf-fugar, is a modern European invention, the difcovery of a Venetian about the end of the 15th, or beginning of the 16th century ; and not practifed in India until very lately.

China boafts, and not without reafon, of the antiquity of her arts and policy over the reft of the Eaft ; as well as over the reft of the world.

world. The ſugar cane is indigenous to China. The climate and ſoil in many parts of Bengal, and other diſtricts of the Eaſt Indies, are alſo ſuitable to the growth and cultivation of the cane; and ſugar is, and we have reaſon to ſuppoſe ever has been, produced there. Nevertheleſs, China is the only country in the Eaſt, even now, where ſugar-candy is made in perfection.

The bright, tranſparent ſugar-candy, ſo beautiful in appearance, and ſo grateful to the taſte, is a peculiar manufacture, and was originally invented in China.

It is exported from China to every part of India, and even to many countries there, where abundance of ſugar is made.

Du Halde ſays, the ſugar of China conſtitutes a great trade to Japan; and that when ſhips go directly from Canton to Japan, the ſugar-candy ſo tranſported yields a profit of a thouſand per cent.

The Chineſe, and all the nations of the Eaſt, ſet no eſtimation on any other ſugar than ſugar-candy. They uſe it in tea, coffee, and all other beverages: and this preference, no doubt, ariſes from judgement, as the fine ſugar-candy is incomparably the moſt delicious ſweet in the world. This may account for the art of refining ſugar into loaf-ſugar never having been practiſed in the Eaſt.

In the ancient, ſteady, and unchangeable empire of China, arts exiſted, while Europe was in a ſtate of barbariſm; arts, which are ſtill the admiration of mankind; and it is probable that this mode of preparing ſugar, ſo well calculated for carriage and preſervation, was practiſed by the Chineſe, and was an article of commerce among them, in much earlier ages than are comprehended in European traditions; which they conſider but as the records of yeſterday.

In reſpect to the derivation of the word *candy*, and when this adjunctive appellation was firſt uſed, to diſtinguiſh *ſugar-candy* from other ſpecies of ſugar, various have been the opinions of the learned.

Some ſuppoſe it had its origin from the iſland of Candia (Crete);—others, from Gandia, a town in Valencia, in which province ſugar was firſt made in Spain *;—others, from the Arabic قند *kand* or *kend*, which ſimply ſignifies ſugar;—and others, from the Latin *candidum (à candore)*, bright, ſhining, white.

* See page 17.

SAL-

SALMASIUS derives it from a corrupt Greek word of the middle ages. He ſays,—

"*Saccharum candum, non à candore dictum, nec à canna; ſed* καντι, *vel* καντον, *&* καντιον, *Græci recentiores vocârunt, quod anguloſum ſit; & quum frangitur, in partes ſemper diſſiliat angulatas. Id Græci vulgares* καντον *appellant.*" Plin. Excert. p. 718.

But this is by no means ſatisfactory; for, if ſugar-candy had this appellation from its angular figure, entire, or broken, the word ſhould be written *cantum*, or *cantium*, in the Latin; or rather *canthum*, or *canthium*; as κανθος is *angulus*, an angle or corner.

SALMASIUS has taken this barbarous word from NICHOLAS MYREPSUS, who wrote his collection of *formulæ*, from the Greek and Arabian authors, about the year 1280: he is one of the lateſt writers in the Greek language. His writings are full of barbariſms, and καντιον is found uſed by him, *De Antidotis*, cap. 35, 94, and 96, to expreſs what the tranſlators have rendered, "*ſaccharum appellatum candum*;"—the ſugar-candy of the moderns.

FUCHSIUS, one of his tranſlators, obſerves, in the notes to cap. 35, and 94, that though the word is *κανϳιον* in the manuſcript copy, and implies what we now call *ſaccharum candi, vel candidum*, yet it ſeems to have been written originally *κανδιον*;—and that *candi* is only an abbreviation of *candidum*.

Now *κανδιον*, I believe, ſtands on no better authority in the Greek language than *κανϳιον*; and I think it is difficult to aſcertain whether the word be a corruption of the Greek *κανθος*, or the Latin *candidum*, conſidering the period when MYREPSUS wrote.

However, I am not inclined to give my ſuffrage to any of the preceding etymons.

May it not have for its origin the Indian word *khand*, from whence the Arabic قند *kænd* is derived, and which is a general appellation for ſugar in Hindoſtan? Sugar-candy is there called *miſree*; white ſugar, *cheenee*; a compoſition they make of ſugar and roſes, *goolkund*; in Arabic گلقند *gülkænd*; a drink made of the ſame materials, *goolſhukure*; the inſpiſſated juice of the cane, *kund-ſeah*, or *jaggery*.

Shukur alſo is a general appellation for ſugar; from which, and the word *khand*, it appears to me, that the others are compounded.

From *ſhukur*, the Indian origin, it is moſt probable that the word ſugar is derived; from thence

thence the Arabians and Perſians had it; سكّر *sükker*, Arab. شكر *ſeker*, Perſ. & Turc. and it has undergone but little variation ſince, in European languages. And, though theſe particulars do not ſeem to have been known to the learned philologiſt, SKINNER, he was certainly right in his conjecture;—*vox (ſugar) proculdubio, ab Indis Barbaricis, cum re tranſlata.*

To conclude this part of my ſubject, I think there can be no doubt but that ſugar-candy was the firſt and only ſpecies of ſugar known to the European antients, and that it was the original manufacture of the Eaſt, particularly of China, the moſt ancient of the Eaſtern nations; and found its way into Europe, as we are certain raw ſugars did in after-ages, when firſt known to Europeans, by the way of India, Arabia, and the Red Sea; ſeveral centuries before MYREPSUS lived.

The Venetians, anterior to the year 1148, imported conſiderable quantities of ſugar from India by the Red Sea, and alſo from Egypt. Sugar was likewiſe made before that time in the Iſland of Sicily. With the produce of this iſland, and the ſugar imported from India and Egypt, the Venetians carried on a great traffic, and ſupplied all the markets of Europe with this commodity *.

* *Eſſai de l'Hiſtoire du Commerce de Veniſe*, p. 100.

Indeed, the Venetian hiſtory informs us, that even prior to 991, when ORSEOLO was Doge of Venice, the Venetians, then forcing their commerce with the Saracens into Syria and Egypt, brought back from thence in return, not only rice, dates, ſena, caſſia, flax, &c. but alſo ſugar *.

This ſhews how much WOTTON was miſtaken, when he aſſerted, that "all the arts and methods of preparing ſugar, which have made it ſo very uſeful to human life, are owing to the modern Portugueſe and Engliſh †."

Doctor WILLIAM DOUGLAS, of Boſton in America, was alſo miſtaken, when, remarking that "the ancient Greeks and Romans uſed honey only for ſweetening, and that ſugar was not known amongſt them," he aſſerts that "PAULUS ÆGINETA is the firſt who expreſsly mentions ſugar ‡."

Doctor CAMPBELL was likewiſe erroneous when he aſſerted, that "the ſugar canes were certainly known to the ancients, though what we call ſugar was not; for, manufacturing the ſweet juice of the ſugar cane into that form was the invention of the Arabians, who beſtowed

* *Eſſai de l'Hiſtoire du Commerce de Veniſe*, p. 71.

† Reflexions upon Ancient and Modern Learning.

‡ Summary Hiſtorical and Political, Vol. I. p. 115. *Anno* 1760.

beſtowed upon it the name it bears, calling it in their own language *ſuccar* *."

The art of refining ſugar was firſt practiſed in England in 1544. The firſt adventurers in this buſineſs were *Cornelius Buſſine*, *Ferdinando Points*, ... *Mounſie*, *John Gardiner*, and Sir *William Cheſter*; theſe perſons were the proprietors of two ſugar-houſes, which were all that were at that time in England †.

The profits ariſing from this concern were at firſt but very inconſiderable; as the ſugar-bakers at Antwerp ſupplied the London market at a cheaper rate than what the Engliſh ſugar-bakers could. After the intercourſe between England and Antwerp was ſtopped, theſe two ſugar-houſes ſupplied all England, for the ſpace of twenty years,; and greatly enriched the proprietors. This ſucceſs induced many others to embark in the ſame trade; a number of ſugar-houſes were eſtabliſhed, and many perſons failed, and became bankrupts.

In 1596, Sir *Thomas Mildmay*, on the pretext that frauds were practiſed in refining ſugar, petitioned queen Elizabeth for a licence, for an excluſive right to refine ſugars, for a term of years; for which monopoly he offered to pay an

* Conſiderations on the Sugar Trade, p. 5. *Anno* 1763.

† Stow's Survey of London, Ed. 1720. vol. II. p. 244.

an annual ſum. His petition however was rejected: and England, which formerly had been ſupplied with refined ſugar from Antwerp, the chief commercial city then in Europe, now not only ſupplied itſelf, but exported great quantities to other countries.

Sugar was taxed by name in England, 2 James II. cap. 4.; prior to that time, it paid twelve pence per pound, or five per cent. poundage, as then was the caſe with all other imported goods.

ON THE PROPERTIES AND USE OF SUGAR.

SUGAR, when firſt introduced into every country, was uſed only medicinally. PLINY leaves no room for doubt on this point. Even in Arabia, in AVICENNA's time, though ſugar was an article of commerce from the Eaſt, there is no record of its being uſed in dietetic, or culinary purpoſes, for ſeveral centuries afterwards,

Sugar was employed originally to render unpleaſant and nauſeating medicines grateful to the ſick: and in pharmacy, in ſyrups, electuaries, confections, and conſerves.

ACTU-

Actuarius was the firſt phyſician who ſubſtituted ſugar for honey in medicinal compoſitions *.

It is not to be ſuppoſed, however, that ſuch a delicious and innocent article could longer be ſubject to the controul of the phyſician, and confined to the apothecary's ſhop, than while the quantity obtainable was inſufficient for the purpoſes of luxury; and the price too great to be admitted, by the generality of mankind, as an ingredient in their food.

As there are but few of the ancients who have even mentioned ſugar, it is not difficult to collect all that has been ſaid of it by them, as to its uſe. It appears nevertheleſs, that it was preferred in their days to honey in medicine.

I have ſaid that Actuarius was the firſt phyſician who uſed ſugar, inſtead of honey, in preſcriptions; becauſe he is ſuppoſed, by me, to have written *anno* 1000; which was before Myrepsus made his compilation; though ſome writers place Actuarius three centuries

* De Pulmonis et cæteris Thoracis Vitiis, lib. IV. cap. 4, lib. V. cap. 1. cap 2. cap. 4. cap 5. cap. 8. He likewiſe mentions the ſugar called *penidii*, lib. V. cap. 6 and 9.—this *penidii*, or *penidium ſaccharum*, is denominated by tho Greek Writers πενίδια.

It is thought to have been a greparation of ſugar, like what we call barley-ſugar.

(anno

(anno 1300) after that period, and ſubſequent to MYREPSUS.

DIOSCORIDES, who is the firſt that mentions ſugar by name, σακχαρον, from which the Latin *ſaccharum* is derived, is alſo the firſt who ſpeaks of the medicinal qualities of ſugar. In his chapter, περι Σακχαρου Μελιτος, he ſays:—

Εστι δε ευκοιλιον, ευστομαχον, διεθεν υδατι και ποθεν· ωφελουν κυστιν κεκακωμενην και νεφρους· καθαιρει δε και τα τας κορας επισκο τουντα επιχριομενον.

"It opens the bowels, and is good for the ſtomach, when drunk diſſolved in water: it relieves pains in the bladder and kidnies: and diſcuſſes thoſe films which grow over the pupil of the eye, and cauſe a cloudineſs in the ſight."

The latter part of this paſſage implies the external application of ſugar. Blowing powdered ſugar, or fine ſugar-candy, into the eyes, has long been a popular practice to remove films, and ophthalmies. Perhaps the practice originated with DIOSCORIDES.

GALEN, in his 7th book of the temperaments and faculties of medicines, περι Μελιτος, ſays,—

Την

Την δυναμιν δε παραπλησιον αυτῳ, καθ' οσον αποῤῥυπτει, και ξηραινει, και διαφορει· καθ' οσον ουτε κακοστομαχον εστιν ως το παρ ημιν, ουτε διψωδες, αποκεχωρηκε της ουσιας αυτου.

"It poſſeſſes ſimilar virtues (to honey), as far as relates to abſterging, drying, and digeſting; however, it is not hurtful to the ſtomach like honey, nor cauſes thirſt: ſo far it differs from honey."

GALEN alſo, in his 8th book of his method of healing, recommends ſugar, among the articles to be uſed, for the regimen of the ſick in fevers.

PAULUS ÆGINETA, *lib.* II. *cap.* 54. recommends, from ARCHIGENES, a piece of "the Indian ſalt, which, in appearance, reſembles common ſalt, but in ſweetneſs honey;" to be kept in the mouth, to moiſten it in fevers.

In the very few preceding authorities we have all that thoſe who are termed the antients have left us on the medicinal virtues of ſugar.

We muſt now take a ſurvey of the confuſed accounts of the Arabians, being the next authorities in ſucceſſion, reſpecting their different ſpecies of ſugar.

I ſhall

I ſhall begin with AVICENNA, and give the Latin verſion of this author. From the reſt of this tribe of copyiſts I ſhall confine myſelf to a few paſſages, which I ſhall give in Engliſh only.

AVICENNA ſays, in his chapter on honey,—

Mel cannarum lenit ventrem, et mel tabazet non lenit. Lib. II tract. 2. cap. 496.

"The honey of canes opens the bowels; but the *tabazet* (the white ſort of honey) does not."

In his chapter expreſsly on ſugar he ſays,—

*Zuccarum quid eſt? Arundo zuccari in natura zuccari exiſtit, et eſt vehementioris lenificationis quàm ipſum. Frigidius eſt album et eſt ſubtilius. Et univerſaliter eſt calidum in fine primi. Et antiquum declinat ad ſiccitatem in primo, et eſt humidum in ipſo; et quanto magis antiquatur, tanto plus exſiccatur. Eſt lenificativum, abſterſivum, lavativum. Et ſulimenum eſt magis lenitivum, et propriè Alfenid**; *imò mel arundinis et zuccarum non ſunt inferiora melle in abſtergendo, et mundificando; et quanto plus antiquatur zuccarum, tanto ſit ſubtilius. Aſſumptum ſicut gumma ab arundine, abſtergit oculum. Lenit pectus,*

* *Penidium Saccharum.*

et

et removet ipſius aſperitatem. Eſt bonum ſtomacho, in quo non generatur cholera: ipſum enim lædit, propterea quia ad choleram convertitur, et eſt aperitivum oppilationum, et in ipſo eſt virtus faciens ſitim, minorem tamen ſitim, quàm facit mel propriè antiquum, et generat antiquum ſanguinem fæculentum, et abſtergit phlegma ſtomachi, et in arundine quidem zuccari eſt juvamentum ad vomitum. Solvit, et propriè illud quod ſuper arundinem invenitur, ſicut ſal, et ſulimenum quidem, et rubeum vehementioris ſunt lenificationis, et quandoque inflat, et quandoque ſedat inflationem, et ipſum quidem cum oleo amygdalino confert colicæ. Lib. II. tract. 2. cap. 755.

AVICENNA, in his chapter de *Aſperitate Linguæ*, copying P. ÆGINETA, ſays, the tongue, when rough and foul in fevers, ſhould be cleanſed with oil of almonds and white ſugar; and after that he ſays,—

Teneat in ore ſuo ſalem qui aſportatur de Indiâ, et eſt in colore ſalis, et dulcedine mellis; et ſumat de eo ſecundum quod dixit ARCHIGENES, *quantitatem fabæ unius.* Lib. IV. fen. 1. tract. 2. cap. 22.

"The ſick ſhould hold in his mouth the ſalt which is brought from India, which is in colour like ſalt, but in ſweetneſs like honey; and he ſhould take of it, according to the directions

directions of ARCHIGENES, the quantity of a bean."

He says again, in his chapter *de Cibatione Febricitantium in generali*,—

Mel cannæ, quod est zuccarum, et proprie mundificatum, melius melle apis, licet ejus abstersio sit minor abstersione mellis. Lib. IV. fen. 1. tract. 2. cap. 8.

"The honey of the cane, that is, sugar, well cleansed, is better than the honey of bees, although its abstersive quality is less than that of their honey."

In his chapter *De Adustione Linguæ*, he advises sugar to be holden in the mouth, to assuage thirst. Lib. III. fen. 6. tract. 1. cap. 19.

AVICENNA further remarks, on the virtues of sugar, compared with honey;—

Quod in Syrupo Acetoso ponatur zuccarum loco mellis; quum zuccarum in abstersione non deficiat à melle plurimum valde; et sic zuccarum minus calidum quam mel, et magis remotum valde, ut convertatur in choleram, quam mel.

Tract. de Syrupo Acetoso.

"That sugar should be used in the syrup of wood sorrel (which was used among the Arabians to make a cooling beverage in the summer time) instead of honey; as sugar is not much inferior to honey in its absterſive property, and is leſs heating; and much leſs ſubject to produce bile."

AVICENNA has a chapter on *Fanid*, or *Penidium*, ſugar; which the tranſlators have rendered *Penidii*; the ſame as before termed *Alfenid*, or *Saccharum Penidium*.

He ſays,—

Penidii, calidi ſunt et humidi in primo, et propriè albi, et ſunt humidiores aliis. Sunt groſſiores zuccaro. Sunt boni tuſſi. Sunt lenitivi ventris. De Penidiis, lib. II. tract. 2. cap. 555.

"The *Penidii* are hot and moiſt in the firſt degree, particularly the white, which are more moiſt than the others. They are larger than ſugar. They are good for a cough. They open the bowels."

RHASES ſays, "ſugar ſoftens the throat and bowels, and does not heat but in a very ſmall degree. Honey is hot, and ſoon converted into bile; but it deſtroys phlegm, and is good for old men of cold habits. In ſummer time, and to thoſe of a hot temperament, honey is hurtful. The *Penidii* are hot; but are alleviating to the throat, bowels and bladder, and warm the parts about the kidneys."

SERAPION,

SERAPION, though he has a ſeparate chapter concerning ſugar, relates only the opinion of others.

He begins with GALEN, and mentions almoſt verbatim what I have already given from that author: particularly that ſugar is not prejudicial to the ſtomach, nor cauſes thirſt, like honey.

From DIOSCORIDES he has given the ſame account I have; that it is a ſpecies of honey found on the canes in India and Arabia: that it is in ſubſtance like ſalt, and brittle between the teeth like ſalt.

From ABEN MESUAI, he ſays, "it opens the bowels, ſtrengthens the ſtomach and cleanſes it, particularly from bile; which it expels by its abſterſive property. The white ſort is not ſo mollifying as the red, and that brought from *Hegen*, like lumps of ſalt.

"The *baoſcer* ſugar ſtrengthens the ſtomach, and is good for pains in the bladder and kidneys, and clears the ſight when uſed in a collyrium; and it dries and reſolves the lax films that extend from the angles of the eyes, over the pupils: when drunk, it does not cauſe thirſt, and on this account it is good in the dropſy, when drunk with the milk of mandragora, or *Laſaba*.

 "New

"New ſugar is hot, and moiſt; and the old hot, and dry. It is good for wind in the bowels, and opens them, and when taken with oil of ſweet almonds, it is good in the colic; and the old ſort is good for phlegm in the ſtomach, unleſs it cauſes thirſt, and generates thick blood. That which is brought from *Aliemen*, and is like maſtich, and is called *haoſcer*, is good for the ſtomach and liver; on account of a ſmall degree of bitterneſs in it: ſugar is good for pains in the bladder and kidneys, and cleanſes them."

From Isaac Bensulaimen he ſays, "the ſugar brought from the region of *Heigen*, and called *haoſcer*, is leſs ſweet than the other ſorts of ſugar, and more drying; for which reaſon it does not remove thirſt like the other ſpecies of ſugar: but it produces good effects in pains of the kidneys, and when drunk in milk of mandragora is good in the dropſy. The milk of the *haoſcer* alſo, when drunk with the milk of mandragora, has the ſame operations, in a greater degree; but it is not ſo ſafe, in habits of hot temperaments."

From Abrianifa he ſays "the *haoſcer* has broad leaves, and has ſugar, which comes out at the buds of the branches, and at the bottom of the leaves; from whence it is collected: in in which ſugar, there is a bitterneſs. The tree bears a kind of apple, about the ſize of an egg, which yields a corroſive liquor. It produces a down, with which pillows and bolſters are ſtuffed. The tree is called *chercha*. When the leaves are cut, the *haoſcer* yields a milk which is collected in the month of May, and ſkins are put in it; and it takes off the hair. The wood of the *haoſcer* is ſmooth, ſtraight, and beautiful; and muſical bards, in their love ſongs, compare the limbs of their miſtreſſes to it."

De Temperament. Simpl. cap. 50.

SERAPION has a chapter alſo from ABEN MESUAI, on the *penidii*, before mentioned, by AVICENNA, and RHASES. It is verbatim from AVICENNA.

Having now ſelected every thing pertaining to ſugar from the Arabians, I ſhall proceed to examine the various opinions of writers in later times, concerning its properties.

The firſt man who took much pains to beſtow a great deal of unqualified cenſure on the uſe of ſugar, was Doctor THEOPHILUS GARENCIERES; the next was our celebrated Doctor THOMAS WILLIS.—SIMON PAULI had preceded them, with his crude notions.

The opinions of theſe phyſicians were adopted, in the infancy of ſugar in England, by Mr. RAY; and the ſentiments of theſe four authors have been diſſeminated in every part of Europe.

GARENCIERES ſays, "*Saccharum et ſaccharata omnia toto genere huic morbo (Tabes Anglica) inſenſiſſima, & in eo progignendo multa eſſe cenſeo quorum quum uſus ſit tam frequens, mirum videri non debet ſi tanta tabidorum ſeges hic pullutat,*" &c.

"*Cum de ſaccharo prædominante qualitate ſit ſermo, illam eſſe caliditatem contendo, quamvis ſatis obſcuram; indicio eſt quod ſitim gignit,*" &c.

"*Qua qualitate calida non parum pulmoni obeſſe poteſt, cum pulmo ſit maximè calidus et moderatè frigidis potius delectetur, calidiorum vero uſu facile inflammationem excipiat,*" &c.

"*Sed quod cardo totius rei eſt, ſaccharum non ſolum temperamento et materia, verum etiam tota ſubſtantia pulmoni eſt inimicum id quod neminem non ignarum mihi negaturum eſſe puto; cum enim non ſolum dulce, ſed etiam ſit dulciſſimum, & propterea amaro è diametro oppoſitum numquid ſequi debet, ſi amarum ex omnium recepta ſententia ſuper vacuos humores ſiccando abſorbet aut detergit, ac propterea optima ratione putredinem arcet, et corpora diu integra conſervat, quod dulce propter oppoſitas facultates, fœcundus*

fœcundus putredinis parens esse debet, id quod etiam longe citius accidet si in partem quæ nulla coctrice facultate prædita sit incidat, à quâ postea non possit edomari? &c.

"*Certum est nullam, vel minimam, fieri fermentationem inter ea quæ qualitatibus inter se conveniunt, ut saccharum et caro, illud enim propter dulcedinem et balsamicam qualitatem, hæc vero ob humorem dulcem, ita ad invicem accedant, ut si caro quæpiam saccharo condiatur, festinam corruptionem patietur, nisi saccharum ad amaritudinem excoctum sit, cum tamen sale condita in multum tempus perseveret, eo quod inter salem qui acris est, et carnis balsamum quod dulce est, quædam fit fermentatio propter dissidium qualitatum, post quam fermentationem novum quoddam temperamentum procedit; idem etiam apparet in saccharo, quod, cum ita cito carnes corrumpat fructus tamen acidos longiuscule à putredine incolumes tutatur, quia ipsius dulcedo cum aciditate seu acerbitate fermentatur, et novum inde temperamentum perfectè mixtum producit. In supradictorum confirmationem non omittendum est, quod in insula Sancti Thomæ sub æquatore moluntcannas, et quod superat, expresso succo, objiciunt porcis qui inde dicuntur in tam miram teneritudinem pinguescere, ut de bonitate cum capris Hispanicis certent, denturque vulgo ventriculis invalidis ad facilem concocturam. Unde*

 colligere

colligere eſt, quod, ſi ſaccharum ea vi et facultate pollet, ut ſuillam omnium fere carnium tenaciſſimam ad tantam teneritudinem adducat, eadem prorſus ratione corruptelam et ſphacelum in pulmonibus accelerabit, cum ipſi ſint molles et ſpongioſæ ſubſtantiæ, et ſtypticis aſtringentibus conſerventur. Luce igitur clarius eſt ſaccharum non alimentum ſed nocumentum, non alexiterium ſed deleterium, eſſe ad Indias rurſus ablegandum, ante quas detectas veriſimile eſt effectum hunc plane latuiſſe, et cum iis mercibus ad nos eſſe advectum." Angliæ Flagellum, ſeu Tabes Anglica. *Anno* 1647. p. 92. & ſeq.

The ſubſtance of which is,—

"Sugar and all kinds of ſweetmeats are very hurtful in conſumption of the lungs; and, as I conceive, the ſo frequent uſe of theſe things tend much to create that diſeaſe; and it is not to be wondered at, that conſumptive complaints are ſo common in England.

"In reſpect to the predominant quality of ſugar, I contend that it is heating, although hidden; and, as a proof of it, it excites thirſt.

"This heating quality of ſugar renders it not a little injurious to the lungs, which are in themſelves very hot; moderately cooling things are

are therefore moſt agreeable to their nature; but heating things eaſily inflame them.

"But the moſt important conſideration is, that ſugar is not only injurious to the lungs in its temperament and compoſition, but alſo in its intire property; which, I believe, no ſenſible perſon will deny; when, from its exceſſive ſweetneſs, it is diametrically oppoſite to the bitter principle, it muſt follow, if bitter things, according to univerſal ſuffrage, abſorb and deterge ſuperfluous humours, expel putrefaction, and preſerve bodies ſound for a great while, that ſweet things, from their oppoſite qualities, muſt be the fruitful parent of putreſcence; and which muſt neceſſarily be more active in their effects when a part is attacked not endowed with the power of concoction; and from which afterwards it is not poſſible to remove the diſeaſe.

"It is certain there is no fermentation, or very little, produced between things which agree in their qualities, as ſugar and fleſh; on account of the ſweetneſs and balſamic quality of ſugar and the ſweet eſſence of fleſh, which aſſimilate with each other; for, if a piece of raw meat be put in ſugar, it ſoon becomes putrid, unleſs the ſugar ſhould have been firſt boiled until all its ſweetneſs is conſumed, and it it has acquired a bitterneſs; but when the meat is put into ſalt, it will be kept from putrifying for a great length of time, from that property in the ſalt which is acrid, and the balſam of the meat which is ſweet, cauſing a kind of fermentation from the oppoſition of their qualities; after which fermentation a certain new temperament ariſes.

" The ſame alſo appears in ſugar, which, though it ſo ſoon corrupts fleſh, yet it will preſerve acid fruits from putrefaction for a long time; becauſe its ſweetneſs ferments with the acidity or ſharpneſs of the fruits, from which a new uniform temperament is produced.

" In confirmation of the preceding obſervations, it is not to be omitted, that in the iſland of *Saint Thomas*, under the æquator, the inhabitants feed their hogs with canes, and the refuſe of the cane juice; from which they are ſaid to fatten, and acquire ſuch wonderful tenderneſs, that their fleſh equals in goodneſs the Spaniſh kids, and is commonly given to people with weak ſtomachs, on account of its eaſineſs of digeſtion.

" From hence we may infer, that if ſugar poſſeſſes the power and property of converting hog's fleſh, the tougheſt almoſt of any animal's, mal's, to ſo great a degree of tenderneſs, for the ſame reaſon it muſt accelerate the decay and ſphacelation of the lungs, when they are of ſuch a ſoft and ſpongy ſubſtance as to require ſtyptics and aſtringents to preſerve them.

"It is therefore clearer than the light that ſugar is not a nouriſhment, but an evil; not a preſervative, but a deſtroyer; and ſhould be ſent back to the Indies, before the diſcovery of which, probably, conſumption of the lungs was not known, but brought to us with theſe fruits of our enterprize."

WILLIS ſays,—

Saccharo condita, aut plurimum imbuta, in tantum vitupero, ut illius inventionem, ac uſum immodicum, ſcorbuti in nupero hoc ſeculo immani augmento, plurimum contribuiſſe, exiſtimem; enim vero concretum iſtud ſale ſatis acri & corroſivo, cum ſulphure tamen delinito, conſtat, prout ex analyſi ejus ſpagyrice facta liquido patet. Quippe ſaccharum, prout ſupra innuimus, per ſe diſtillatum, exhibet liquorem aqua ſtygia vix inferiorem; quod ſi ipſum, in veſica plurima aqua fontana perfuſum, diſtillaveris, quamvis ſal fixus non adeo aſcendit, prodibit tamen liquor inſtar aquæ vitæ acerrimæ, urens, ac ſumme pungitivus; cum itaque

*itaque ſaccharum, quibuſvis ferè alimentis commixtum, ita copioſe a nobis aſſumitur, quam veriſimile eſt, ab ejus uſu quotidiano, ſanguinem & humores, ſalſos et acres, proindeque ſcorbuticos, reddi? Author quidam inſignis** TABIS ANGLIÆ *cauſam in immoderatum ſacchari apud noſtrates uſum retulit: neſcio an non potius etiam hinc ſcorbuti increbreſcentis fomes derivetur.* De Scorbuto, cap. 10. Anno 1674.

"I ſo much condemn all things that are preſerved with ſugar, or have much ſugar mixed with them, that I conſider the invention, and immoderate uſe of it, in this preſent age, to have very much contributed to the immenſe increaſe of the ſcurvy.

"For it plainly appears, by the chemical analyſis of ſugar, that this concrete conſiſts of an acrid and corroſive ſalt; but tempered with a portion of ſulphur.

"Sugar, diſtilled by itſelf, yields a liquor ſcarcely inferior to *aqua fortis*; but, if it be diluted plentifully with water, and then diſtilled, although no fixed ſalt will aſcend, yet there will come a liquor like the ſharpeſt brandy; hot, and highly pungent.

* He alludes to GARENCIERES.

"Therefore

"Therefore it is very probable, that mixing ſugar with almoſt all our food, and taken to ſo great a degree, from its daily uſe, renders the blood and humours ſalt and acrid; and conſequently ſcorbutic.

"A certain eminent author * attributes the cauſe of the frequency of conſumptions of the lungs, in England, to the immoderate uſe of ſugar. I am not certain whether alſo the fomes of the increaſing ſcurvy may not rather be derived from thence."

RAY ſays,—

Antiquiores medici, qui ſuperiore ſeculo vixerunt, unanimi fere conſenſu ſaccharum ad pectoris & pulmonum vitia, raucedinem, tuſſim, gutturis aſperitatem, lateris & thoracis ulcera, commendant. Cæterum apud nos in Anglia non ita pridem in crimen adduci, & magna infamia laborare cæpit, medicis tum noſtratibus, tum extraneis, ſcorbuti & tabis popularium morborum præter ſolitum graſſantium nuperas furias, immoderato in cibis & potu ſacchari uſui imputantibus †. *Et, ne quis humidiori potius æris conſtitutioni eas peſtes ſuſpicetur; in Luſitania (aiunt) regione calida ob eandem rationem tabes epidemica facta eſt. Lu-*

* GARENCIERES.

† WILLIS and SIMON PAULLI.

ſitani

ſitani enim plus ſacchari conſumunt quam quævis alia gens præter Anglos.

De ſcorbuto iidem antiquiores, quos diximus, medici cum recentioribus conſentiunt, eum à ſacchari nimio uſu produci, cum dentibus valde nocuum, nec eos nigros duntaxat reddere, ſed & putreſcere & vacillare & exidere facere ſaccharum ſcribant, quæ certa ſcorbuti ſigna & ſymptomata ſunt. Saccharum enim ſalem acidum & maxime corroſivum continere ex diſtillatione patet. Scorbutus autem ſali fixo in ſanguine redundanti debetur, proinde iis quæ ſale volatili abundant ſanatur. Hiſtoria Plantarum, lib. XXII. cap. 3. p. 1279, 1280, Anno 1688.

"The phyſicians who lived in the laſt century, with unanimous conſent, recommend ſugar for complaints in the lungs, hoarſeneſs, cough, rawneſs of the throat, and internal ulcerations: yet, among us in England, not long ſince, it began to be accuſed, and to labour under great diſcredit, by our own, as well as foreign phyſicians, who impute the ravages which the ſcurvy and conſumption have lately made in England to the immoderate uſe of ſugar in our food and drinks.

"No perſon ſhould therefore attribute theſe evils to the moiſture of the atmoſphere; for, they

they ſay, that in Portugal, where the air is warm, conſumption of the lungs is there epidemic, from the ſame cauſe; as the Portugueſe uſe more ſugar than any people, except the Engliſh.

"In regard to the ſcurvy, the ſame more ancient phyſicians, as well as thoſe of later times, agree, that it is produced by the too great uſe of ſugar; and that it is very hurtful to the teeth, and not only renders them black, but cauſes them to decay, and to looſen in their ſockets, and to fall out; which are certain ſigns and ſymptoms of ſcurvy.

"Sugar alſo contains an acid and very corroſive ſalt; which appears from diſtillation.

"The ſcurvy is cauſed by a redundant fixed ſalt in the blood; and is therefore cured by ſuch things as abound with a volatile ſalt."

From theſe extracts it appears, that GARENCIERES and WILLIS were the founders of the ſect of Antiſaccharites.

I have been more extenſive in my quotations from theſe writers than I ſhould have been, if it were not that I wiſh to preſent the reader with that jargon of GARENCIERES, and abſtruſe and obſolete theory of WILLIS, which have been conſidered as ſtanding authority by many

many ſubſequent writers; and quoted in academic diſſertations, in the ſchools of medicine.

In Willis's time, according to his account, and his account is true, almoſt every perſon had, or fancied he had, the ſcurvy.

He ſays,—

Nunc fere omnes eo laborant, aut ſe laborare putant.

The ſcurvy at that time made great ravages in England; beſides which, the faſhion of the day gave to the ſcurvy, all the minor ſtraggling indiſpoſitions that were deſtitute of adoption.

Conſumption of the lungs, and every other ſpecies of ſcrophula, are endemial in England. Scurvy is the ſame. This diſeaſe, which made ſo much havoc in the laſt century, is now ſcarcely known in England.

The ſcurvy, like any ſporadic diſeaſe, may have its revolutions, and appear and diſappear in the character of an epidemic. I do not ſpeak of ſcurvy acquired by local and particular cauſes.

It is incredible that Willis and Ray, two well-informed men, ſhould not know that the deſcription of people moſt afflicted with the ſcurvy, at all times, and in every country, is that, which ſeldom taſte any ſugar.

It

It is not leſs extraordinary that the learned WILLIS ſhould refer to ſo ſuperficial an authority as GARENCIERES; or the laborious RAY, to the weak effuſions of SIMON PAULLI.

The rhapſody of GARENCIERES is entirely his own; but what WILLIS advances has a better ſtamen, but it is not his own. It is taken from ANGELUS SALA, whom he has not mentioned, and from whom he has made a partial ſelection, merely to ſupport his favourite theory of the ſcurvy.

SALA enumerates many evils which may ariſe in weak habits and bad conſtitutions from the *exceſſive*, and what he terms the *abuſe* of ſugar; ſuch as, debility of digeſtion; loſs of appetite; blackneſs and looſening of the teeth; offenſive breath; colic; lax bowels; bilious, ſcorbutic, and hyſterical complaints.

But let it be remarked, that it is to the inordinate uſe of ſugar, among already diſeaſed people, to which SALA attributes theſe evils.

For, his own reflexion on the occaſion is, that "the exceſſive uſe of the moſt excellent and ſalutary things is always hurtful to the human frame."

SALA, however, views the ſubject with impartiality, if not with judgement; and does ample juſtice to the wholeſome properties of ſugar.

Sacchari virtutes ac operationes, ſecundum rationem & modum uſurpati, ſunt ſequentes :—Corpus nutrit, ſanguinem probum generat, ſpiritus vitales recreat, ſemen auget, fœtum in utero firmat ; quod nemo miretur, ſiquidem hoc ſubjectum, æmulam vini dulciſſimi virtutem, ut porro docebo, in ſe complectitur, cujus proprietatem, in refectione longo morbo emaciatorum, ſenum, melancholicorum, moderatus uſus comprobat ; conducit affectibus faucium, pulmonum, raucedini, reſpirandi difficultati, ex defluxione acri obortis, exulcerationi item pulmonum, laterum, renum, veſicæ, puriſque ex iiſdem expurgationi ; inteſtinorum aſperitatem lenit, eorumque excrementa emollit, & expulſioni apparat ; vulnera in corpus penetrantia & puncturas, ut etiam oculorum maculas, extergit ; dolores ulcerum & tumorum, humores influxos coquendo, aut ſi ad ſuppurationem inhabiles ſunt digerendo, diſſipat ; pluresque alios in medicina uſus habet, brevitatis gratia prætermittendos. Saccharologiæ, part I. cap. 6. anno 1637.

" Sugar, uſed in a proper manner, nouriſhes the body, generates good blood, cheriſhes the ſpirits, makes people prolific, ſtrengthens children in the womb ; and this is not aſtoniſhing, becauſe becaufe it contains fimilar virtue to the very fweet wines; which property is fhewn by the effects, produced by the moderate ufe of fugar, in reftoring emaciated people, after long ficknefs; and ftrengthening the aged, and low-fpirited weak people.

"It is ferviceable alfo in complaints of the throat, and lungs; hoarfenefs, and difficulty of breathing, arifing from an acrid defluxion; for ulcerations of the lungs, cheft, kidneys, and bladder; and to cleanfe thofe parts from purulent matter.

"It eafes pains of the inteftines, foftens the fæces, and prepares them for expulfion; it cleanfes wounds and punctures in the body; alfo films in the eyes.

"It removes pains in ulcers and tumours, by concocting the flux of humours; or, if they have no tendency to fuppuration, by difperfing them."

What I fhall further felect, together with the preceding, will fhew the eftimation in which fugar has been held, by learned men, at different periods, in different countries; and will embrace all that relates to it deferving notice.

Baptista Porta, who, in point of date, was much earlier than the authors before mentioned, muſt not be omitted; becauſe his opinion of ſugar was the prevailing one, prior and down to his time, all over Europe. Beſides, as he lived at Naples, the uſe of ſugar was better known to him, at that period, than to any contemporary writer in the northern parts of Europe; where it had then ſcarcely entered into dietic uſe. He ſays,—

Ex harundinibus ſaccharum extrahimus, non ſolum id incorruptibile, ſed aliis præſtat ne corrumpantur; vulneribus injectum à putrefactione liberat; ex eo ſolo ingentia vulnera ſanari vidimus. Sit igitur familiare ſaccharum vitam prolongare cupientibus, quia nec humores, nec cibum in ventre putreſieri, permittit. Phytognomica, lib. V. cap. 1. p. 201. anno 1560.

"Sugar, extracted from canes, is not only incorruptible in itſelf, but preſerves all other things from corruption; ſprinkled upon wounds it keeps them from mortifying. I have ſeen very large wounds cured only with ſugar *. Therefore ſugar ſhould be conſtantly

* The method of treating freſh wounds among the Turks, is, firſt to waſh them with wine, and then ſprinkle powdered ſugar on them. The celebrated Monſieur Belloste cured obſtinate ulcers with ſugar diſſolved in a ſtrong decoction of walnut leaves. This I have found to be an excellent application.

uſed

ufed by thofe who wifh to prolong life; be-caufe it will not fuffer the humours, nor the food, in the body to putrify."

POMET fays, "The white and red fugar-candy are better for rheums, coughs, colds, catarrhs, afthmas, wheezin s, than common fugar; becaufe, being harder, they take longer time to melt in the mouth, and keep the throat and ftomach moifter than fugar does. Put into the eyes, in fine powder, it takes away their dimnefs, and heals them being bloodfhot; it cleanfes old fores, being ftrewed gently on them." *Hiftoire général des Drogues*, *Lib.* II. *cap.* 38, *anno* 1694.

LEMERY gives nearly a fimilar account of fugar; but fays it is hurtful to the teeth. and caufes vapours. *Traité univerfel des Drogues Simples*, *anno* 1693.

HERMANN fays, "Sugar confifts of a fweet foft mucilage, and an agreeable fharpnefs; from whence it becomes an aliment as well as a medicine. The Indians boil it in water with a fmall quantity of flower for nourifhment. It promotes urine, and is fpecific in coughs, hoarfenefs, fharp humours, and other difeafes of the lungs.

 "It

" It ſhould not be uſed in large quantities by the melancholic, hypocondriacal, and hyſterical, nor by people in fevers, on account of its proneneſs to aſceſcence.

" With fat broth and *ſal gem*, it is uſed in glyſters for children; and it is alſo given to them, newly born, to relax the bowels, with oil of ſweet almonds.

" Taken with oil of ſweet almonds, it is a remedy for pains in the bowels. It is an excellent vulnerary and balſamic, reſiſting putrefaction; it is good for putrid ulcers, and abſterges clouds and films in the eyes. It is hurtful to the ſcorbutic, and to ſuch as are ſubject to bilious còlics. It is hurtful alſo to the teeth and gums; rendering the breath offenſive, and the teeth black and rotten. In glyſters it is good againſt worms, and is alſo an anthelmintic remedy taken by the mouth." *Cynoſura, vol.* I. *p.* 704 *& ſeq. anno* 1710.

Boerhaave ſays,—

" Sugar never generates phlegm, but, on the contrary, diſſolves it. Neither does it increaſe the bile, or is converted into it; but opens, attenuates, and divides it. At the ſame time, by diſſolving the oleaginous particles in the body, it may induce leanneſs; and, by too much attenuation,

attenuation, produce debility, and too great laxity. For which reaſon, it is often found hurtful to the ricketty and ſcorbutic." *Element. Chemiæ, vol.* II. *p.* 260, *anno* 1724.

Geoffroy ſays,

" Sugar, taken moderately with food affords good nouriſhment. It promotes concoction, if after a full meal a lump of it be eaten.

" Almoſt all phyſicians recommend it in complaints of the cheſt and lungs. A lump of ſugar or ſugar-candy, held in the mouth, ſoftens the acrimony of the phlegm, aſſuages coughs, and relieves rawneſs in the throat and fauces; as the ſugar, ſo melting and ſwallowed, forms with the ſaliva a defence to the parts.

" It promotes expectoration, particularly if reduced to the conſiſtence of a ſyrup with the oil of linſeed, or ſweet almonds. Taken in this manner, it alſo eaſes the colic and pains in the bowels, and aſſuages the gripes in children.

" Drinks, ſweetened with ſugar, cleanſe the cheſt, and eaſe coughs by correcting the phlegm; they remove hoarſeneſs, cleanſe ulcers of the lungs, force the urine, open the bowels, and are ſalutary in the pleuriſy and peripneumony.

"But, if taken alone in a great quantity, it is hurtful, and particularly to bilious people. It ferments in the ſtomach and inteſtines, excites wind, and, by its fermentation, produces bile; and, by attenuating, renders it more fluid. Hence ſugar and ſweet things are ſaid to create bile.

"From the ſaline ſpiculæ of ſugar, the bile is rendered more acrid; from which an heat is not only kindled in the bowels, but alſo in the whole body, and is carried into the maſs of blood.

"It creates worms in children.

"It is hurtful to the teeth, cauſing blackneſs and ſcales, and making them looſe. Therefore, always after uſing much ſugar, it is proper to rinſe the mouth and teeth carefully.

"Nothing, however, is to be feared from the moderate uſe of ſugar; but, on the contrary, we find that an agreeableneſs is added to our diet, by which the ſtomach is diſpoſed to perform a proper digeſtion of the food; and the gaſtric fluid and the aliments are aſſiſted, for the neceſſary fermentations, both in the ſtomach and the bowels; from whence the beſt quality of the blood, and other humours of the body depending on the firſt concoction, is produced." *De Vegetabilibus*, *Sect.* I. *Art.* 9, *anno* 1741.

In

In taking a ſurvey of the writers on ſugar, it is impoſſible to overlook Dr. FREDERICK SLARE; whoſe unqualified praiſes of the virtues of ſugar may be properly oppoſed to the unqualified cenſures beſtowed on it by GARENCIERES and WILLIS. Neither muſt honeſt old LIGON be forgotten.

"Sugar," ſays LIGON, "has a faculty to preſerve all fruits that grow in the world from corruption and putrefaction; ſo it has a virtue, being rightly applied, to preſerve us men in our healths."

"Dr. BUTLER, one of the moſt learned and famous phyſicians that this nation or the world ever bred, was wont to ſay;—

If ſugar can preſerve both pears and plumbs,
Why can it not preſerve as well our lungs?*

"And, that it might work the ſame effect on himſelf, he always drank in his claret wine great ſtore of the beſt refined ſugar; and alſo preſcribed it ſeveral ways to his patients, for

* The Doctor might have been a famous phyſician; but much is not to be ſaid here, for his rhyme or his reaſon. The old adage is not left far behind by the Doctor;—

That which preſerveth apples and plumbs,
Will alſo preſerve liver and lungs.

colds,

colds, coughs, and catarrhs; which are diseases that reign in cold climates, especially in islands, where the air is moister than in continents." *History of Barbadoes, anno* 1673.

SLARE says,—" I have a strong and home argument to recommend the use of sugar to infants; of which to defraud them is a very cruel thing, if not a crying sin. The argument I bring from Nature's first kind tribute, or intended food for children, so soon as they are born; which is, that fine juice or liquor prepared in the mother's breasts, called breast-milk, of a fine delicate sweet taste. This sweet is somewhat analogous, or a taste agreeable, to sugar; and, in want of this milk, it is well known, sugar is brought to supply it. You may soon be convinced of the satisfaction which a child has from the taste of sugar, by making two sorts of water-paps, one with, and the other without, sugar; they will greedily suck down the one, and make faces at the other. Nor will they be pleased with cow's milk, unless that be blessed with a little sugar, to bring it to the sweetness of breast milk.

" I will set down an experiment I had from a friend. He was a little lean man, who used to drink much wine in company of strong drinkers.

drinkers. I aſked him how he was able to bear it. He told me that he received much damage in his health, and was apt to be fuddled, before he uſed to diſſolve ſugar in his wine; from that time he was never ſick nor inflamed, nor fuddled with wine. He uſually drank red wine.

"I made uſe of ſugar myſelf in red wine, and I found the like good effect; that it prevents heating my blood, or giving my head any diſturbance, if I drink a larger portion than ordinary.

"I allow about two ounces of ſugar to a pint of wine; and dare aſſert that this proportion will take off the heating quality of wine in a good meaſure; and, after one has ſome time uſed himſelf to add ſugar to his wine, he will be pleaſed with the taſte, and feel the comfortable and cordial virtue of this compoſition.

"Let thoſe that are thin, and apt to have hot hands and heated brains upon drinking wine, and cannot abſtain or be excuſed from drinking, take notice of this counſel, and try it for ſome time; and they will be pleaſed with the delicious taſte, and ſalubrious effects, of this ſaccharine addition." *Vindication of Sugars, anno* 1715.

SUGAR,

Sugar, analytically examined, demonſtrates phlegm, ſpirit, acid, and oil; and, by fermentation, yields an ardent ſpirit.

Two pounds of refined ſugar produced one ounce and thirty-ſix grains of a limpid, inodorous, inſipid phlegm; twelve ounces and ſix drams of a liquor at firſt limpid, then browniſh and empyreumatic, then acid, and then urinous; and ſix drams of thin browniſh oil.

The black reſiduary maſs in the retort weighed eight ounces, two drams, and three grains; which, calcined in a furnace for fifteen hours, left one ounce, one dram, and ten grains, of brown cinders; from which two drams and forty grains of a fixed alcali ſalt were obtained by lixivium.

In the diſtillation there was a loſs of eight ounces and ſix drams; in the calcination, ſeven ounces and fifty-three grains.

Sugar is an eſſential ſalt, conſiſting of an acid ſalt, oil, and earth. It ſhews no ſigns of acid or alcali. It takes flame, and burns brightly. It diſſolves eaſily in aqueous menſtrua, but not in ſpirituous or oily. Diſſolved in in water, it undergoes fermentation, and acquires firſt a vinous, then an acetous flavour.

If one pound of ſugar be diſſolved in ſix or eight pints of water, and a ſpoonful of the yeaſt of beer be added to it, and well mixed, and expoſed to gentle heat, in a veſſel properly cloſed, but the veſſel muſt not be full, in a few hours it will begin to ferment with great vehemence; and in three or four weeks, more or leſs, according to the quantity of liquor, and warmth of the ſituation where it is placed, it will produce a ſtrong vinous liquor, not unlike honey and water. This liquor diſtilled yields a ſtrong ardent ſpirit. If the whole fermenting materials be expoſed longer to a continued heat, a ſtrong vinegar, like that of wine, will be produced; by the liquor changing from its vinous to its acetous ſtate.

Among more recent chemical inveſtigation, and in the higher elementary branches of chemical ſcience, diſcoveries have been made important to arts and manufactories: and alſo for the œconomical purpoſes of life. Sugar has not eſcaped that ſcrutiny, which the magnitude of ſuch a ſubject demanded.

The

The renowned BERGMAN gives us the following new and interesting obſervations:

"Sugar being juſtly conſidered as an eſſential ſalt, it will readily be granted, that it contains an acid; this acid may be ſeparated, and exhibited in a cryſtalline form, by the following proceſs:—

"(A) Let one ounce of the pureſt ſugar, in powder, be mixed, in a tubulated retort, with three ounces of ſtrong nitrous acid, whoſe ſpecific gravity is nearly 1,567.

"(B) When the ſolution is completed, and the moſt phlogiſticated part of the nitrous acid has flown off, let a receiver be luted on, and the ſolution gently boiled. In this proceſs an immenſe quantity of nitrous air is diſcharged *.

"(C) When the liquor acquires a dark-brown colour, let three ounces more of nitrous acid be poured on, and the boiling continued until the coloured and ſmoking acid has entirely diſappeared.

"(D) Let the liquor in the receiver be then poured into a larger veſſel; and, upon cooling, ſmall quadrilateral priſmatic cryſtals are

* In order to procure this acid, common aqua-fortis will ſerve as well as the ſtrongeſt nitrous acid; and any glaſs, thin enough to bear a moderate heat, will do as well as a retort.

found

found adhering together, at an angle generally of about 45 degrees: theſe, collected and dried on bibulous paper, weigh 109 grains.

"(E) The remaining lixivium, boiled again in the ſame retorts, with two ounces of nitrous acid, until the red vapours begin to diſappear, upon cooling, as before, affords 43 grains of ſaline aciculæ.

"(F) If to the viſcid glutinous liquor which remains, there be added, at different times, ſmall quantities of nitrous acid, amounting in all to two ounces, by boiling and evaporating to dryneſs, a ſaline maſs is at length formed, brown, glutinous, and deliqueſcent, which, when perfectly dried, weighs half a drachm; but in depuration nearly half of this weight is loſt.

"(G) The cryſtals obtained in the manner above deſcribed, are to be depurated by repeated ſolution and cryſtallization; an operation which is particularly neceſſary to the portion got, as deſcribed in (F).

The laſt lixivium (F), digeſted with nitrous acid, and evaporated to dryings by the ſun's heat, exhibits priſms ſimilar to thoſe mentioned, (D) and (E); ſo that this affords a method of abridging the number of depurations.

"(H)

" (H) To obtain, therefore, one part of this ſalt, there are required 3 of ſugar, and 30 of nitrous acid. Thus it may be reckoned among the moſt expenſive ſalts hitherto known.

" It muſt be particularly obſerved, that a much ſmaller quantity of cryſtals will be obtained, if the boiling be continued ever ſo little beyond the proper time.

" (I) The acid thus obtained I call *acid of ſugar* ; not becauſe it is procurable from that ſubſtance only, but becauſe ſugar affords it more pure, and in greater quantity, than any other matter hitherto tried.

" Thus 100 parts of gum arabic, treated as above, with 900 of nitrous acid, at the beginning of the boiling foam violently, and, upon cooling, yield ſcarce more than 21 of ſaccharine acid, priſmatically cryſtallized ; but at the ſame time the ſolution, even to the laſt, ſeparates a ſaccharated lime, which, when collected, weighs 11, and contains about 5 of the acid of ſugar : 8 parts of highly-rectified ſpirit of wine, with 24 of nitrous acid, yield 3 of ſaccharine acid, but, for the moſt part, in a ſquamous form, and loaded with much moiſture ; beſides, honey, and whatever ſubſtance contains ſugar, in the ſame way, produces the ſame

ſame acid; and although acid of tartar, diſſolved and boiled in nitrous acid, in the ſame manner, yields a ſalt ſomewhat ſimilar to this, both in taſte and ſquamous cryſtillization, yet it is of a whiter colour; and, beſides, is unchangeable in the fire, yielding only a coal as before.

" In another diſſertation it will be ſhewn that the acid of ſugar occurs alſo in animal ſubſtances.

" This ſalt poſſeſſes many properties; ſome peculiar to itſelf, ſome common to it with other acids, though differing more or leſs in degree: and theſe we are now to conſider.

" (A) The cryſtals have an exceeding pungent taſte; but a ſolution of theſe, when ſufficiently diluted, excites a very agreeable ſenſation on the tongue. Twenty grains communicate a ſenſible acidity to a quart of water.

" (B) It makes red all the blue vegetable juices, except that of indigo. A ſingle grain diſſolved in four ounces of water inſtantly makes red the blue paper for covering ſugar-loaves; which is not affected by the weaker acids: and twelve grains, diſſolved in a quart of water, produce the ſame effect upon paper tinged with turnſole.

" (C) It attacks alkalis, earths, and ſundry metals; and diſſolves them with effervefcence, if they be united with aërial acid. Theſe combinations ſerve to diſtinguiſh this evidently from all other acids."

Saccharated Lime *.

" Eighty-two parts of ſaccharine acid take up 100 of pellucid calcareous ſpar, but not immediately; becauſe the ſurface, when ſaturated with the acid, prevents the acceſs of the acid to the internal nucleus. Nitrated lime is completely precipitated by acid of ſugar, in the form of a white powder, not ſoluble in water.

" Of 119 parts, by weight, of this powder, 72 fall to the bottom, and 47 appear upon evaporation: hence it is ſhewn, that 100 parts contain, of acid 48, of pure lime 46, and of water 6; ſo that not only the preſence of lime in water is diſcovered by acid of ſugar, but even its quantity may, without difficulty, be aſcertained.

" The ſaccharine acid attacks lime with ſuch force that it ſeparates it from every other: this combination,

* This ſection is of importance to manufacturers of ſugar, and analyſers of waters.

combination, therefore, cannot be decompoſed by any acid, alkali, or earth, hitherto known, and can only be decompoſed by fire.

" Hence alſo we underſtand the neceſſity of lime-water in the purification of ſugar; for, the juice of the cane contains a ſuperabundance of acid, which prevents the dry concretion; and even if to pure ſugar diſſolved in water be added the ſaccharine acid, it will not form cryſtalline grains.

" Now, nothing more powerfully attracts this acid than lime; and, when united with it, it is inſoluble, and either falls to the bottom, or floats in the ſcum. Lime-water, therefore, affords the moſt complete means of effecting the cryſtallization; as it removes the impediment, and, beſides, may eaſily be added in any proportion, without communicating any heterogeneous matter.

" Many perſons have thought that a portion of the lime remains mixed with the ſugar; but, if the purification be properly conducted, the nature of the ingredients, the circumſtances of the operation, and, finally, the moſt accurate analyſis, abundantly ſhew, that there is not the ſmalleſt trace of lime remaining.

" Good ſugar diſſolves totally in diſtilled water; which could not poſſibly be the caſe if

 there

there were present any lime, either crude or united with the saccharine acid; as either of these substances, whether alone or mixed with sugar, is utterly insoluble in water *.

" The vegetable alkali does indeed absorb the acid of sugar, but forms with it a salt not very difficult of solution; and, besides, a caustic lixivium, if used in too great a quantity, will dissolve a portion of the sugar. In saccharated lime, the earthy basis predominates: for, when boiled with syrup of violets, it strikes a green colour.

" If we consider the nature of the acid of sugar, we shall find that it does not resemble the nitrous acid in any other instance than those properties which are common to all acids; besides, it expels the nitrous acid from lime, terra ponderosa, magnesia, and metals; yielding to the other acids nothing but alkalis; while the nitrous acid produces salt, either deliquescent or easily soluble, acid of sugar yields such as are scarcely soluble in water.

" Alkalis, when nitrated, detonate with ignited phlogiston; but, when saccharated, shew not the least signs of deflagration, which they

* The idle opinions respecting lime, used in manufacturing sugar, are here completely refuted. Lime holds the first place, in an eminent degree, in the elective attractions of the acid of sugar.

evidently

evidently do upon the addition of the ſmalleſt particle of nitrous acid.

"The nitrous acid corrodes tin and antimony, but ſcarcely diſſolves them; while acid of ſugar readily acts upon them: phlogiſticated nitrous acid, united with vegetable fixed alkali, deliqueſces, does not form cryſtals, and is readily expelled by vinegar, or even by acid of ſugar, ſtill more loaded with phlogiſton: all which circumſtances by no means take place with reſpect to the fixed vegetable alkali united with acid of ſugar.

"Many other diſſimilarities will occur upon compariſon; ſo that theſe acids are of a nature not only unlike, but in many inſtances diametrically oppoſite.

"If any will attribute all the difference to phlogiſton, I will not deny that that ſubtile principle forms a wonderful ſource of difference; but the difference which takes place here can by no means be attributed to this, when properly examined.

"The nitrous acid is weakened, and made far more volatile, by union with the phlogiſton; the acid of ſugar much more fixed, even when loaded with ſo great a quantity as to be cryſtallizable; it almoſt every where expels the ſtrongeſt nitrous acid, as experiments ſhew;

besides, the phlogisticated nitrous acid produces, with the very same matters, compounds totally different from those with acid of sugar.

" Nothing can be judged from circumstances which are unknown, forged, or, at best, possible: and among all the facts yet known, concerning the acid of sugar, we can find no signs of its being derived from the nitrous acid.

" However, let us enquire more deeply; let us principally consult nature, not indifferently and slightly, supplying the deficiencies with fiction, but candidly and properly, by apt and accurate experiments; otherwise her answers, like those of the oracles of old, will be either delusive or ambiguous.

" But, by whatever means the acid of sugar is produced, it must be considered as distinct, and different from all others, being always essentially and specifically the same. Its singular properties, some of which are of considerable use in chemistry, shew that it deserves the most particular attention.

" From the time of STAHL, many considered the nitrous and marine acids as generated from the vitriolic; but, if all confiding in this theory (which yet is contradicted by daily observation) had neglected the examination of those acids,

acids, confidering them as fubordinate and derivative, we fhould be to this day ignorant of many fingular facts, which, by degrees, were difcovered; principally becaufe many confidered thefe acids as diftinct and feparate fubftances *."

The faccharine matter, fays the illuftrious DE FOURCROY,—" which many chemifts confider as a kind of effential falt, is found in a great number of vegetables; and may be properly ranged among their immediate principles.

" The maple, the birch, the red beet, the parfnip, the grape, wheat, &c. contain it. MARGRAFF extracted it from moft vegetables. The petals of many flowers, and the necta-

* Abbé FONTANA has obtained an acid perfectly like that of fugar, and faccharine fubftances, from all gums and refins. Mr. WATT, of Birmingham, found by adding nitrous acid to galls, and conducting the procefs in the way recommended by profeffor BERGMAN, that thefe aftringent bodies contain the acid of fugar in greater abundance than the fubftance from which it derives its name. Mr SCHRIKEL obtained an acid from galls by diftillation, but very different from BERGMAN'S; as may be feen in SCHEEL'S effays. To obtain acid of fugar, without vital air, or nitrous acid, would be a fact of great importance in the prefent ftate of chemical theory.

 riums

riums placed in these organs, elaborate a principle of this kind.

"The sugar cane, *arundo saccharifera*, contains it in larger quantities, and affords it more readily, than any other plant.

"Sugar consists of a peculiar acid united to a small quantity of alkali, and much fat matter. It crystallizes in hexahedral truncated prisms: and in this state is called sugar-candy. By distillation it affords an acid phlegm, and a few drops of empyreumatic oil. The residue is a spungy light coal, which contains a small quantity of vegetable alkali. This salt is inflammable. On hot coals it melts, and swells up very much, emits a penetrating vapour, and becomes converted into a brown yellow matter. It is very soluble in water, to which it gives much consistence, and constitutes a kind of mucilage, called syrup. Syrup diluted with water is capable of fermentation, and affords ardent spirit.

"Bergman has obtained, from all saccharine matters, especially sugar, an acid of a peculiar nature.

"Though, at the time of the first discovery of this acid, it was thought that the saccharine principle was necessary for its formation *, it

* *Manna* affords an acid of the same nature.

it is at prefent known, that a great number of vegetables, which are not faccharine, afford it in greater abundance : fuch are gums, ftarch, vegetable gluten, falt of forrel, lemon juice, fpirit of wine, and animal matter, as M. BERTHOLLET has difcovered.

" Among thefe fubftances, thofe which produce the greateft quantity of this peculiar acid, by the action of fpirit of nitre, are fuch as do not afford fugar.

" Pure fugar did not afford BERGMAN more than one third of its weight of acid ; and M. BERTHOLLET obtained more than half, from wool.

" It feems, therefore, as M. DE MORVEAU thinks, that this acid is formed by the union of a peculiar attenuated oil, which exifts in all organic fubftances, and is the fame throughout ; and that confequently the name of faccharine acid is improper.

" SCHEELE has obferved that the acid of lemons chryftallized by the procefs defcribed by BERGMAN, does not afford faccharine acid by treatment with nitrous acid ; though lemon juice itfelf affords it. The vitriolic acid, employed for the purification of this acid of fugar, feems therefore to decompofe the oil which forms the bafe of the faccharine acid."

The

The ſaccharine principle of grapes, berries, and fruits, is the baſis of their reſpective wines; therefore almoſt every deſcription of wine may be imitated by art, from ſugar.

The wines of France, Italy, Spain, and Portugal, particularly of the two laſt countries, are not only adulterated, but ſucceſsfully counterfeited from ſugar.

They who underſtand perfectly that part of the manufacture which belongs to colouring the liquor, and giving it the eſſential characteriſtic of the relative vegetable flavour, can deceive people of no mean judgment, and ſell them a caſk of wine "*neat as imported.*"

Of other vegetable juices abounding with ſugar, LEWIS has given the following deſcription, in his tranſlation of NEWMANN'S chemiſtry:

"In ſome parts of North America, particularly in Canada, a kind of ſugar is prepared from the juice which iſſues upon wounding or boring certain ſpecies of the maple tree, one of which is named from hence the ſugar-maple; as alſo from the wild or black birch, the honey locuſt,

locuſt, and the hickery. The maple is moſt commonly made uſe of for this purpoſe, as being the richeſt, and as beſt enduring the long and ſevere Winters of that climate. The juice is boiled down, without any addition, to a thick conſiſtence, then taken from the fire, kept ſtirring until its heat is abated, and ſet in a cold place, where the ſugar quickly concretes into grains, reſembling common brown powder ſugar.

" The trees are tapped early in the Spring, about the time the ſnow begins to melt. It is obſervable, that when the weather begins to grow warm they bleed no more; and that after the bleeding has ſtopped they begin to run again upon covering the roots with ſnow. The more ſevere the Winter has been, the juice is found to be richer, and in greater quantity. The trees which grow on hills, or high land, yield a richer juice than thoſe which are produced in low countries; and the middle-aged than the young or old.

" Mr. Kalm informs us, in the Swediſh Tranſactions for the year 1751, that one tree, if the Summer does not come on haſtily, will yield about forty-two gallons of juice, Engliſh meaſure: and that the quantity which iſſues in one day is from three to ſix gallons; that eleven gallons

gallons of juice of middling quality give a pound of ſugar, and that a pound has been gained from three gallons and an half. That two perſons can, in one Spring, prepare commodiouſly two hundred pounds. He obſerves, that this ſugar is weaker than that from the ſugar-cane; and that it is reckoned that a pound of common ſugar goes as far in ſweetning as two pounds of maple ſugar.

"The large maple, commonly called ſycamore-tree, bleeds alſo in Europe; from which an actual ſugar has been prepared. In the Tranſactions above mentioned, for the year 1754, there is an account of ſome experiments made in this view upon the Swediſh maple. Eight trees, none of them under thirty years, bled, in four days, fourteen gallons of juice, which inſpiſſated gave two pounds and an half of brown ſugar. Another time, the ſame eight trees bled, in three days, ten gallons and an half, which yielded one pound four ounces of ſugar, with half a pound of ſyrup. It is the ſaccharine juice of the maple-tree, which, exuding from the leaves, renders them ſo apt to be preyed upon by inſects.

"The common birch bleeds alſo a large quantity of ſweetiſh juice, which yields, on being inſpiſſated, a ſweet ſaline concrete, not however

however perfectly of the faccharine kind; but feeming to approach more to the nature of manna.

"There are fundry other vegetables, raifed in our own country, which afford faccharine concretes; as beet-roots, fkirrets, parfneps, potatoes, celery, red cabbage-ftalks, the young fhoots of Indian-wheat. The fugar is moft readily obtained from thefe, by making a tincture of the fubject in rectified fpirits of wine; which, when faturated by heat, will depofit the fugar upon ftanding in the cold *."

We have now fome rational data concerning the real principles of fugar; from which it may be fuggefted, that it has not even yet been fo fully inveftigated, but that it may be applicable in many ways, more than we are at prefent acquainted with, to a variety of interefting purpofes.

But, before I proceed in the obfervations I have to offer the public on the dietetic and medicinal ufes of fugar, it may be proper to

* Sugar is alfo obtainable from grapes; particularly from dried raifins. We frequently find large grains of pure fugar among *Malaga* raifins, that have lain long compreffed together.

fubmit

ſubmit ſome remarks, the reſult of my literary reſearches, to the learned and curious. This may contribute to ſettle many vague notions and erroneous opinions relative to the heraldry of ſugar, and the cane, of which it is the produce.

I have before obſerved, that the ancient Grecians and Romans had no knowledge either of the ſugar-cane, or of ſugar.

For, there is no mention made of the SUGAR-CANE among the Grecian writers, until an hundred years after HIPPOCRATES; nor among the Roman writers, until the time of POMPEY'S expedition into Syria.

SUGAR is not mentioned by either Grecian or Roman writer until the time of NERO. Neither poet nor hiſtorian mentions it in the Auguſtan age.

In the diſtricts of Aſia, inhabited by the Hebrews and Iſraelites, at the time that country was traverſed by the Grecians and Romans, ſugar was there unknown.

There is no record among the Jews, even ſo late as at their diſperſion, on this ſubject.

From the writers on the expedition of the Cruſaders but little is to be collected reſpecting the ſugar-cane, and leſs of ſugar; notwithſtanding ſugar had been a commercial article for

for centuries prior to that memorable epoch of insanity *.

In the writings of MOSES, and in many parts of the Bible written by others, we find the word קנה.

This word, passing into the Arabic language, قناة *kænat*, is the immediate origin of *canna*, a cane. *Pl.* قنا *kænā* — *cannæ*, canes.

But this קנה in the Bible has many significations.

As a verb in the Hebrew, it imports to buy; procure; possess. קָנָה *kanah* he bought; he procured; he possessed. קָנֶה *kaneh* as a noun, a spear †; a staff ‡; a reed, or rush §; a balance ||; bone of the arm ¶; branches of the candlestick in the temple **.

It is said by several writers, that by קנה, in some places in the Bible, the *sugar-cane* is meant; and consequently that this plant was known to the antient Hebrews. This is to

* *Histoire du Commerce de Venise*, p. 71, 100.

† *Psalms*, lxviii. v. 30. קינן *hastæ*. 2 *Samuel*, c. xxi. v. 16.

‡ *Ezekiel*, c. xxix. v. 6.

§ *Isaiah*, c. xix. v. 6, 7. and c. xlii. v. 3. 1 *Kings*, c. xiv. v. 15, 2 *Kings*, c. xviii. v. 21. *Job*, c. xl. v. 21. *Ezekiel*, c. xl. c. xli. c. xlii. c. xlv.

|| *Isaiah*, c. xlvi. v. 6.

¶ *Job*, c. xxxi. v. 22. the *ulna*.

** *Exodus*, c. xxv. v. 32.

our

our preſent purpoſe, and the firſt object of inquiry.

In five places only, in the Bible, this word occurs, as a noun, implying an article, or vegetable production; to which any uſe, or application, is aſſigned as ſuch.

Theſe places are in *Exodus*, c. xxx. v. 23. *Canticles*, c. iv. v. 14. *Iſaiah*, c. xliii. v. 24. *Jeremiah*, c. vi. v. 20. and *Ezekiel*, c. xxvii. v. 19.

If we examine the paſſages here referred to, we ſhall find that קנה has been doubtfully interpreted at beſt; evidently erroneouſly in ſome inſtances; and in none is it poſſible that the *ſugar cane* could be meant by it.

In the preceding chapter in *Exodus* we find,—

קִנְּמָן בֶּשֶׂם—קָנֶה בֶשֶׂם

Kinnemon beſem,—kaneh beſem.

This is rendered in the Septuagint verſion,

Κινναμωμον ευωδες—καλαμος ευωδης.

The Latin verſions in the Polyglotts have it,

Cinnamomum odoriferum, and *calamus odoriferus.*

In

In our Englifh Bible it is, " fweet cinnamon and *fweet calamus*."

In fome of the Latin verfions the קְנֵה בֹשֶׂם is rendered *calamus beneolens*, and *calamus aromaticus*.

Again, in the *Canticles*, both *kaneh* and cinnamon are mentioned, as diftinct articles;

קָנֶה וְקִנָּמוֹן

Καλαμος και κινναμωμον *.

The Latin verfions have this, *calamus aromaticus et cinnamomum*; and *fiftula et cinnamomum:* קָנֶה is alfo rendered *canna* in one verfion of the Polyglott †, as it is in MONTANUS ‡. Our Englifh Bible has it " calamus and cinnamon."

In *Ifaiah*, this *kaneh* appears to be highly grateful to Jehovah, who is reprefented by him as being angry with the Ifraelites, for neglecting their burnt offerings and facrifices.

לֹא קָנִיתָ לִּי בַכֶּסֶף קָנֶה

In our Englifh Bible this paffage is,—

* C. iv. v. 14.

† WALTON. *Interpret. interlin. à* PAGNINO.

‡ *Ibid.*

"Thou haſt bought me no *ſweet cane* with money *."

This is the paſſage which has miſled ſo many people: from *kaneh* being erroneouſly rendered *ſweet cane.*

Jeremiah repreſents Jehovah, as being angry with the Iſraelites; and will not receive their burnt offerings, and ſacrifices. Here alſo the *kaneh* is mentioned by Jehovah, as an article of the firſt conſideration.

וְקָנֶה הַטּוֹב מֵאֶרֶץ מֶרְחָק

The whole verſe is thus rendered in the Engliſh Bible.

"To what purpoſe cometh there to me incenſe from Sheba? *and the ſweet calamus from a far country?* Your burnt offerings are not acceptable to me, nor your ſacrifices ſweet unto me †."

The Septuagint has the part of the verſe I have quoted from the Hebrew, *κινναμωμον εκ γης μακροθεν.* "CINNAMON *from a far country.*"

* C. xliii. v. 24.
† C. vi. v. 20.

In

In the Latin verſions it is rendered *calamus ſuaveolens de terra longinqua*; and *cinnamomum de terra longinqua*; and *calamus aromaticus de terra longinqua.*

It is neceſſary to obſerve here, that, in the Septuagint, קָנֶה is converted into *κινναμωμον*, *cinnamon*; which word is not in the original text; and the epithet טוֹב *tōb*, good, perfect, beſt, is entirely omitted.

Theſe are errors in the labours of thoſe great men, who firſt took the Hebrew Bible out of the hands of the Jews, and gave all that is known of it to poſterity.

But theſe errors have led ſome writers, who knew no more of קנה than what they obtained from this paſſage in the Bible, to ſuppoſe it was a ſynonyme for cinnamon.

In *Ezekiel*, we find the *kaneh* enumerated by Jehovah, among the boaſted commodities of merchandize at Tyre, in her moſt flouriſhing ſtate of commerce.

קִדָּה וְקָנֶה בְּמַעֲרָבֵךְ הָיָה׃

"Caſſia and *calamus* were in thy market *."

In *Exodus*, *kaneh* is mentioned by Moses as one of the four ſpices in the *Holy Anointing Oil*;

* C. xxvii. v. 19.

which, he ſays, Jehovah ordered him to make in the following manner:

"* Take thou unto thee, principal ſpices of pure myrrh 500 ſhekels; ſweet cinnamon and *ſweet calamus*, of each 250 ſhekels; caſſia 500 ſhekels; and of olive oil an *hin*. And thou ſhalt make it an oil of Holy Ointment, to be made an ointment compound, after the art of the apothecary †."

With this *Holy Anointing Oil*, MOSES ſays, he was directed by Jehovah to anoint the tabernacle, the ark of the teſtimony, the tables, the veſſels, the candleſticks, the altar of incenſe, the altar of burnt offering, and the laver and his foot, that they might be ſacred; he was alſo ordered to anoint AARON and his ſons, and conſecrate them, that they might miniſter in the prieſts office; and it was to be an *Holy Anointing Oil* for the children of Iſrael throughout their generations.

MOSES, in this remarkable chapter, mentions alſo the other compoſition, ſo venerated by the Iſraelites. This is the *Holy Perfume*; which, he ſays, Jehovah directed him to make in the following manner, for perfuming the Tabernacle. "Take unto thee ſweet ſpices, ſtacte,

* C. xxx. v. 23.

† רֹקֵחַ an apothecary, or compounder of ſweet ointments.

and

and onycha, and galbanum; theſe ſweet ſpices, with pure frankincenſe, of each ſhall there be a like weight."

"And thou ſhalt make it a perfume, or confection, after the art of the apothecary, tempered together, pure and holy *."

This *Perfume*, like the *Holy Oil*, was not to be uſed for profane purpoſes, nor even to be imitated. For, whoſoever ſhould attempt to make either, or put any of the oil on a ſtranger, or ſmell to a perfume compounded in a ſimilar manner, was, MOSES ſays, by Jehovah's decree, to be "even cut off from his people."

The ancient Jews delighted in ſpicey odours. MOSES made fumigation, and the uſe of aromatic drugs, part of their religion.

They uſed them even in their beds;—

נַפְתִּי מִשְׁכָּבִי מֹר אֲהָלִים וְקִנָּמוֹן׃

"I have perfumed my bed with myrrh, aloes, and cinnamon †."

The ingredients they uſed were indeed coarſe, but wholeſome. By fumigation and perfumes, they corrected the foul air in their tabernacles, and other places where many dirty

* V. 34, 35.

† *Proverbs*, c. vii. v. 17. Engliſh Bible.

people were crowded together; by which means diſeaſes were prevented.

This doctrine of fumigation is one of the many excellent leſſons in the Bible, which has been much neglected.

It ſeems to have ariſen from perverſeneſs among Chriſtians, hatred to the Jews, and diſreſpect to MOSES, who knew all ſciences, and was an excellent phyſician, that they have profited ſo little by ſeveral wiſe practices, as well as precepts, in the Bible. The papiſtical Chriſtians, it is true, burn frankincenſe in their churches; but it is chiefly near the altar, whe e the prieſt only is benefited by it.

The Chriſtians in England cleanſe their houſes and public places by water, heated air, and ventilation; and hence it is we have to lament, that often the beſt Chriſtians die of conſumptions.

In England the Chriſtians are much cleaner than they uſed to be. They would now call a man,—

"Miſbeliever, cut-throat dog, and ſpit upon his gaberdine *,"

if he were to adviſe their taking an hint for purifying their perſons, or places of devotion, after the manner of the Iſraelites.

* *Shylock.*

But

But I muſt finiſh my obſervations on *kaneh*.

What this קָנֶה was, I know not. It could not be the *acorus*, or *calamus aromaticus*; that was too plentiful to be ſo valued; and grew in Syria, Arabia, and the iſlands of the Gentiles, and in all the ſwamps and marſhes in the adjacent countries to the land of Iſrael; and was not brought מֵאֶרֶץ מֶרְחָק "from a far country."

That the *kaneh* was ſome ſpicey produce of a tree, concretion, bitumen, wood, bark, or gum, is certain; and it is alſo certain that it was not only aromatic, but precious, from the epithets given to it, and from its uſes among the choſen people, and the eſtimation in which it was ſaid to be holden by Jehovah himſelf.

The epithet בֶּשֶׂם imports *ſpicey*, *ſweet ſcented*, not *ſweet taſted*; therefore the *ſugar cane* is entirely out of the queſtion.

The *ſugar cane* does not yield a fragrant ſmell, naturally or burnt. Neither will it keep ſound, when ripe, after it is cut; but will periſh like the ſtalk of a cabbage plant; and could not be preſerved from rotting in a paſſage "from a far country *."

* Neither did cinnamon come "from a far country." That was the produce of Arabia. "Habet India, quæ Auſtralis eſt, cinnamomum ſicut Arabia." STRABO, lib. XV.

How קָנֶה ſhould have been rendered *calamus*, ſo univerſally as it has been, I cannot conceive.

The authors of the Septuagint tranſlation of the Bible muſt have underſtood, from the time and countries in which they lived *, the Hebrew language better than any people at this day. But here they have miſguided their implicit followers; and, indeed, this is not the only inſtance where they were not ſo correct as they ſhould have been.

We find among the Greek writers *καννα*, *δοναξ*, and *καλαμος*; and among the Roman writers *canna*, *arundo*, and *calamus*;—but theſe names are uſed indiſcriminately for a *cane*, or a *reed*.

This has been the cauſe frequently of miſunderſtanding theſe writers; where the context has been inadequate to ſettle a preciſe and determinate meaning.

The *γλυκοκαλαμος*, in later times of NICHOLAS MYREPSUS, which his tranſlators have rendered *dulcis calamus repurgatus*, is the pulp of the *caſſia fiſtula* †.

* About 227 years before the Chriſtian æra.

† *De Antidot. Sect.* 1. *c.* 449. *anno* 1280.

It

It has been ſaid, by ſome writers, that the word שכר in the Bible has an alluſion to ſugar.

This word, like קנה according to the conſtruction of the Hebrew language, has ſeveral ſignifications; but none whatever that has any relation to ſugar.

As a verb, it imports to drink to exceſs; to be drunk; to hire for wages; to reward. שָׁכַר *ſhakar*, or *ſhacar*, he drank to exceſs; he was drunk. שׂכַר *ſachar*, he hired for wages; he rewarded.

As a noun, it has various meanings; but is chiefly uſed for ſome exhilarating, ſtrong, and intoxicating liquor. Our Engliſh Bible every where denominates it, "ſtrong drink."

The Septuagint renders it *σικορα**, *σικερα*†; the Latin verſions *ſechar*, *ſicera*.

Moses ſays, Jehovah ordered him to proclaim to the children of Iſrael, that "when either man or woman ſhall ſeparate themſelves to a vow, *a vow of a Nazarite*, he ſhall ſepa-

* *Numbers*, c. vi. v. 3. *Iſaiah*, c. xxix. v. 9.

† *Numbers*, c. xxviii. v. 7.

rate

rate himſelf from wine, and שֵׁכָר *(ſhecar) ſtrong drink*; and ſhall drink no vinegar of wine, or vinegar of שֵׁכר *(ſhecar) ſtrong drink*; neither ſhall he drink any liquor of grapes, nor eat moiſt grapes, or dried *."

The inſpired prophet JEREMIAH ſays, Jehovah gave him "the cup of his fury;" and that he "made all nations drink of it, to whom the LORD had ſent him;" and he ſaid unto them, "drink ye, *and be* וְשִׁכְרוּ *(veſhikru) ye drunken*, and ſpue, and fall †."

Theſe paſſages are here given, the original Hebrew words excepted, from the Engliſh Bible †; which, though not an elegant, is in this inſtance a faithful tranſlation of the Hebrew.

What ſottiſh liquor שֵׁכָר *ſhecar* was, no perſon knows. It was probably made from grain; perhaps from honey.

The moſt wild and barbarous nations have ever had the art of making intoxicating liquors to get drunk with, by ſome proceſs of fermentation, from ſaps of trees ‡, fruits §,

* *Numbers*, c. vi. v. 3.

† *Jeremiah*, c. xxv. v. 27.

‡ *Palm*, *Birch*, *Laudan*, *Sycamore*, &c.

§ *Apples*, *Pears*, *Cherries*, *Currants*, *Gooſeberries*, *Plums*, *Mulberries*, *Elderberries*, *Blackberries*, *Ocaijba*, &c.

and

and grain * ; and from roots, and other natural productions of different countries.

The ſugar cane, though indigenous to latitudes within and near the torrid zone, arrives at excellence only in the hotteſt climates. But much rain, or water, as well as ſun, is neceſſary to its maturity.

When we conſider that the ſaccharine principle is the ſoul of vegetable creation, and ſee how ſparingly it is diffuſed through the general productions of the earth; and how little is collected from the wide range of flowers, by the conſummate ſkill of the laborious bee; or from roots, trees, fruit, and grain, by the chemic art; we cannot but admire the partiality of Nature to the luſcious CANE, her favourite offspring, the ſublimeſt effort of heat and light.

The proportion of ſugar to the cane juice, depends on the quality of the cane †. We conſider a pound of ſugar from a gallon of cane juice, as good yielding; and three hogſheads of ſugar, of 14 cwt. each, from an acre of land, as ample produce. But for this quan-

* *Wheat, Barley, Oats, Millet, Rice, Maize, Teca,* &c.

† See p. 23.

tity,

tity, the ſoil muſt be good, and the canes of the firſt year's cutting, and in perfection.

In the proceſs of refining muſcovado ſugar, a ton weight, of good quality, gives the following products :—

	Cwt.	q.	lb.
Double, and ſingle refined ſugar,	9	1	$5\frac{5}{16}$
Piece ditto, ...	4	0	0
Scale, or baſtard ditto, . . .	2	0	0
Melaſſes, or treacle, ...	4	1	22
Scum, and dirt, ...	0	1	$0\frac{11}{16}$
	20	0	0

That ſugar is nutritious in the moſt eminent degree has been long known. It is the baſis of all vegetable nutrition.

Every root and earthly production is nutritious, in proportion to the ſaccharine principle it contains. Nothing nouriſhes that is entirely free from this ſaccharine principle ; otherwiſe, turnips would be as little nutritive as cucumbers, being, like them, the ſugar excepted, ſcarcely any thing but water.

Milk is nutritious on the ſame account ; and that milk is moſt nutritious which moſt abounds with ſaccharine ſweetneſs ; and when milk is defective in this quality, from bad paſturage and

and other caufes, our vegetable fugar fhould be added to it, to remedy fuch defect.

In all cafes fugar helps the affimilation of milk in the ftomach; and not only prevents its curdling, and difordering that organ, but corrects the tendency which milk has to injure the breath, by adhering to the teeth and gums, and rendering them foul and offenfive.

There are many people to whom a milk diet would be a great convenience and gratification; and there are fome habits of body and diforders wherein it would often be of the utmoft utility; but the ftomach frequently is unable to bear it. Here fugar is the only means to reconcile the difagreement.

A learned and worthy relation of mine, having been much afflicted with the gout, and having feen the good effects of a milk diet in fimilar cafes to his own, wifhed to have recourfe to it in the fame manner, and make it a principal part of his fuftenance; but he could not. It curdled, and became four, heavy, and difgufting in his ftomach. He was always very fond of milk, but never could ufe it without inconvenience, even when he was a boy.

However, on reading the former edition of this work, he was determined to have another

trial

trial of milk, with the addition of ſome ſugar. This ſucceeded, and he now makes two meals every day entirely on milk and bread, with great pleaſure and comfort; and with infinite advantage to his health.

As milk has the property of injuring the teeth, and is much uſed in ſchools, and conſtitutes great part of the ſuſtenance of moſt young people, a tooth-bruſh and water ſhould always be employed; or at leaſt the mouth ſhould be well rinced with water, after a meal made of milk.

No modern phyſicians have noticed this; but the ancients were well acquainted with the injurious effects of milk, on the teeth and gums *.

In regard to ſugar being prejudicial to the teeth, this has long been known as a prudent old woman's bug bear, to frighten children; that they might not follow their natural inclination, by ſeizing opportunities, when they

* P. Ænigetæ, lib. I. c. 86. Lac gingivas & dentes lædit. Quare poſt ipſum acceptum, primum aqua mulſa, deinde vino adſtringente, os colluere oportet.

Oribasii à Galeno Medicin. Collect. lib. II. c. 59.—Mirum in modum uſus lactis frequens dentes & gingivas lædit, nam gingivas flaccidas, dentes putrefactioni & eroſioni obnoxios facit: ergo ſumpto lacte, os vino diluto colluendum eſt; erit etiam accommodatius ſi mel eidem adjicias.

are

are not watched, of devouring all the ſugar they can find.

This ſtory has had a good effect among the common people in Scotland. They are impreſſed with a notion that *ſweeties* hurt the teeth; therefore they live contented without an article, not always within the compaſs of their finances.

Slare, and many others, uſed ſugar as a principal ingredient in tooth powders. It is a component part of many paſtes, and other dentrifices; and what the French call *opiates*, for the preſervation of the teeth and gums.

When milk is not the ſole diet of children at their mother's breaſt, ſugar, in various mixtures and vehicles, makes the chief portion, eſſentially, of their ſupport.

Sugar affords great nouriſhment, without oppreſſing their tender powers of digeſtion. The nutritive principle of their natural food, is thus happily imitated.

Sugar does not create worms in children, as has been often ſaid: on the contrary, it deſtroys worms. Some writers have mentioned this *; but my authority is my own obſervation.

* *Act. Med. Leip. anno* 1700.

In

In the Weſt Indies, the negro children, from crude vegetable diet, are much afflicted with worms. In crop-time, when the canes are ripe, theſe children are always ſucking them. Give a negro infant a piece of ſugar cane to ſuck, and the impoveriſhed milk of his mother is taſteleſs to him. This ſalubrious luxury ſoon changes his appearance. Worms are diſcharged ; his enlarged belly, and joints diminiſh ; his emaciated limbs increaſe ; and, if canes were always ripe, he would never be diſeaſed.

I have often ſeen old, ſcabby, waſted negroes, crawl from the *hot-houſes*, apparently half dead, in crop-time ; and by ſucking canes all day long, they have ſoon become ſtrong, fat, and ſleaky.

The reſtorative power of ſugar, in waſted and decayed habits, is recorded by ſeveral phyſicians, in different parts of the world. I have known many people, far advanced in pulmonary conſumption, recovered by the juice of the ſugar cane.

A friend of mine, a clergyman in Shropſhire, has favoured me with a very intereſting account of a cure performed by the uſe of ſugar, in ſuch a diſeaſed ſtate of the lungs, as

is

is generally denominated a complete consumption.

The case is curious; and I shall recite as much of it as is necessary to the fact. The patient is a gentleman, and a neighbour of my friend. He had been attended by two eminent physicians who had given up the case as incurable. He then applied to the late Doctor JAMES, who ordered one paper of his powder to be divided into eight parts, and one part to be taken every other night, diluting with strong green tea. After being a week under this treatment, he was taken out of his bed every morning between nine and ten o'clock, and supported by two persons, was hurried along the garden-walk, when the weather was fine, which brought on expectoration, and retching; when the oppression from his lungs was removed by these operations, he was put into his bed again, and had a tea-cup full of milk-warm mutton broth given him; this excited a gentle perspiration, and pleasant sleep. He was allowed calves feet, chicken, fish, and a glass or two of port wine. This was JAMES's practice.—The patient thought himself benefited by it.—He was at this time so reduced that he kept his bed upwards of two months, not being able to stand; nor even to ſit upright in a chair without ſupport; his cough was violent, with bloody purulent ſpitting, fever, and profuſe, and ſudden night ſweats. He was then twenty-ſix years of age.

His diſorder originated from ſleeping with his bed-room window open, in the month of June, 1770; and increaſed to an alarming degree by the month of Auguſt; and in March, 1771, the above phyſicians gave over all hopes of his recovery. Theſe things premiſed, I ſhall give the gentleman's own words, in anſwer to ſome particulars ſtated to him, by my deſire.

"I did not take to the uſe of ſugar, until I was reduced to ſo weak a condition as to be unable to take any thing elſe. Sugar was never preſcribed for me by any phyſician; but being very thirſty, from the fever, I had a great inclination for ſpring water; which I was not permitted to have, by the affectionate relative who nurſed me, without ſome Muſcovado ſugar, a little ginger, and a piece of toaſted bread in it. I ſoon became extremely fond of the ſaccharine taſte, and uſed to ſweeten the water to exceſs. I did not take it as a medicine, nor confine myſelf to any ſpecific quantity; but always uſed it, when my appetite

appetite or inclination ſeemed to require it. However, I at length uſed it in a conſiderable quantity; ſome days to the amount, I believe, of eight ounces; and that, with the ſmall portion of toaſted bread put into my drink, was the principal part of my ſuſtenance during the greater part of twelve years; nor did it ceaſe to be ſo until my ſtomach became ſtrong, and capable of bearing animal food."

He continued in good health from the preceding period until the month of April, 1793; when, in conſequence of a neglected cold, he had a return of all his former dangerous ſymptoms; but, by recurring to his old regimen, he was again reſtored to health, in about ſix months time, excepting in ſtrength; which he recovered by degrees. He is now in better health than he ever was before in his life.

Fontanus, Valeriola, and Forrestus, aſſert that they had patients cured of conſumptions of the lungs by a continued uſe of the *conſerve of roſes*; and Reverius knew an apothecary who cured himſelf of a confirmed conſumption by almoſt living on the conſerve of roſes. Avicenna records an inſtance of a ſurpriſing cure performed on a patient, ſo nearly dying in a conſumption, that prepa-

 rations

rations were making for her funeral; and who was not only perfectly reſtored to health, but became very fat, by eating a great quantity of conſerve of roſes *. Foreign journals are full of hiſtories of conſumptions cured by this medicine.

There are inſtances where people have ſcarcely taken any other nutriment than conſerve of roſes. Some have eaten a pound, and a pound and an half, of this conſerve every day: *three fourths of this conſerve are ſugar.*

The virtues of ſugar are not confined to its nutritive and balſamic qualities. It reſiſts putrefaction, and preſerves all ſubſtances,—fleſh, fruits, and vegetables,—from corruption.

It has a great ſolvent power; and helps the ſolution of fat, oily, and incongruous foods and mixtures. It promotes their maceration and digeſtion in the ſtomach; and qualifies

* This curious caſe deſerves to be remembered. "*Si non timerem dici mendax, narrarem in hac intentione mirabilia, & referrem ſummam, qua uſa eſt mulier phthiſica. Pervenit res cujus ad hoc, ut ægritudo cum ea prolongaretur adeo, donec pervenerit ad mortem, & vocaretur ad ipſam, qui præpararet ea, quæ mortui ſunt neceſſaria. Tunc quidam frater ejus ſurrexit ad eam, curavit eam, hac cura tempore longo, & revixit & ſanata eſt, & impinguata eſt; & non eſt mihi poſſibile, ut dicam ſummam ejus, quod comedit de Zuccaro Roſaceo.*" Lib. 3. fen. 10. tr. 5. c. 6. p. 668.

the

the effects of digeſtion, to the powers of the lacteals *.

For this reaſon, ſugar is much uſed in foreign cookery, and ſo much introduced at the tables of the luxurious in France, and alſo in Italy, Portugal, Spain,—and indeed in every country, excepting England, in confections, preſerves, ſweetmeats, and liqueurs †.

Sugar, in the form of ſyrup, is an admirable vehicle, to comminute and convey to the internal abſorbing veſſels any alterative, mineral, or vegetable medicine.

By its miſcible property, it diffuſes minutely any preparation it may hold in ſolution, or

* "*Nous penſons qu'il donne aux alimens une ſaveur qui diſpoſe l'eſtomac à une coction plus parfaite, qui augmentant la force du levain ſtomacal, excite une fermentation plus complette des alimens dans l'eſtomac & dans les inteſtines, & qu'il contribue par conſéquent à entretenir dans le chyle, dans le ſang, & toutes les humeurs, les qualités néceſſaires pour accomplir & maintenir les fonctions. Ce qui depend toujours de la premiere digeſtion, dont le dérangement eſt le principe de tous ceux qui arrivent dans le corps humain.*" POUPPE DESPORTES, vol. III. p. 375.

"*Acria lenit, acida obtundit, ſalſa mitiora auſtera ſuaviora reddit, fatuis & inſipidis gratum ſaporem tribuit; atque ut uno verbi concludam, omnium ſaporum domitor videri poteſt; nihilque abſque ſaccharo ferè ventri gratum, panificio operi additur, vinis miſcetur. aqua enim ſaccharo ſuavior, ſalubriorque redditur.*" NONNII, de Re Cibaria, lib. I. c. 47. p. 152.

† "*Si perquam, parce ultima menſa devoretur, concoctionem juvat, ſatietatem ferè tollit.*" ALEX. PETRONIUS, De Victu Romanorum, p. 328.

 union,

union, on the ſurface of the ſtomach and inteſtines; and ſubjects it to the capacity of the orifices of the ſmalleſt veſſels.

Sugar alone has many medicinal virtues; and, made into a common ſyrup with water, and diſguiſed, and perhaps ſomewhat improved by vegetable additions, has performed many cures in diſeaſes, from impoveriſhed blood, rickets, and ſcrophula, that have baffled the moſt ſkilful phyſicians; and empiricks have accordingly availed themſelves of what they term ptiians, and medicated ſyrups.

The balſamic and fattening properties of ſugar are prominently viſible in all parts of the world where it is made; and not confined to the human race.

The celebrated hiſtorian Mr. BRYAN EDWARDS was too accurate in his reſearches, to ſuffer a fact, ſo intereſting as this, to eſcape his obſervation.

In his Hiſtory of the Weſt Indies, he has drawn a faithful repreſentation of a plantation, in the ſeaſon of making ſugar *.

He ſays, — "ſo palatable, ſalutary, and nouriſhing is the juice of the cane, that every individual of the animal creation, drinking

* January, February, March, and April.

freely

freely of it, derives health and vigour from its uſe. The meagre and ſickly among the negroes exhibit a ſurpriſing alteration in a few weeks, after the mill is ſet in action. The labouring horſes oxen, and mules, though almoſt conſtantly at work during this ſeaſon, yet being indulged with plenty of the green tops of this noble plant, and ſome of the ſcummings from the boiling houſe, improve more than at any other period of the year *."

It muſt be obſerved, that muſcovado, or what is called moiſt ſugar, is laxative; and that, in uſing the juice of the cane, either as a luxury or a medicine, this alſo is of a laxative nature, particularly with people unaccuſtomed to it; and ſometimes it operates as an active purgative, and diſorders the bowels. This happens frequently to Europeans, who arrive in the ſugar countries juſt at crop-time, and, allured by its grateful novelty, take it to exceſs.

It has been already remarked, that when vegetable ſugar was firſt known, it was uſed only in medicine; that it was then preferred to honey, and in proceſs of time almoſt entirely ſupplanted honey; the ſweet, which had

* Vol. II. p. 221, 2d edit.

been in uſe among mankind, coeval with natural hiſtory.

The ſuperiority of ſugar would ſoon be diſcovered by obſerving phyſicians, as being exempt from the uncertain, and ſometimes dangerous effects of honey.

There are many people whom a tea-ſpoonful of honey will diſorder. In ſome habits, even that quantity will cauſe violent pains in the ſtomach and bowels; and will act as an emetic, or cathartic, or as both. In others, honey will cauſe eryſipelas, nettle raſh, itching, and a general ſwelling in the body and limbs, and occaſion ſuch deleterious effects, as are produced by ſome vegetable *fungi*; ſome kinds of fiſhes, muſcles, and poiſonous plants.

Medical men who have travelled, or read, or have had much experience, know what extraordinary effects reſult from theſe cauſes.

A melancholy inſtance among many I have ſeen, of the miſchievous effects of muſcles, lately occurred, in the neighbourhood of Chelſea Hoſpital; where a boy of ſeven years old was deſtroyed by eating them: and his father eſcaped the ſame fate, with great difficulty, after vomiting of blood, and convulſions.

The

The caufe of what is confidered as the poifon of mufcles is generally fuppofed to arife from fome malignant quality inherent in the fifh itfelf; according to the place where it is found, and particular feafons. Some fuppofe the poifon confifts in a kind of *ftella marina*, a fea infect, frequently found in mufcles; whofe fpawn is very corrofive, and when applied to the fkin excoriates it.

But the real caufe is, in the indigeftible property of a part of the mufcle, which fhould never be eaten; and without which, mufcles are innocent and nutritive.

The noxious part of mufcles is the hard threads, or wiry filaments, by which they faften themfelves to one another; to the bottom of fhips; and to rocks, and ftones; and, as if anchored by the ftrongeft cable, no waves nor current can break their hold.

Thefe filaments iffue from an hard cartilaginous fubftance, at the root of what is commonly called the tongue of the mufcle, in the middle of its body.

That honey fhould fometimes produce the ill effects I have mentioned cannot create furprize; if we reflect that the bee diftils from every flower, in the great unweeded garden of Nature;

Nature; and that the quality of his manufacture depends on the quality of his materials.

Hence it is that honey in different countries differs ſo much in flavour, and conſequently in wholeſomeneſs.

The honey of ſome countries is poiſonous to every one who makes uſe of it. POMPEY loſt three regiments in *Pontus*, poiſoned by honey*; and PLINY ſays, there is a diſtrict in that country, which yields honey that makes people mad who eat it.

But the peculiar antipathy to honey, the occaſion of theſe remarks, may be excited by the eſſential property of ſome particular vegetable in that multifarious compound; or, moſt probably, by the nature of the compound itſelf.

Incredible as the fact may appear, I know a perſon who cannot touch honey with her finger, without immediate nervous affections, and cold ſweats; and, what is ſtill more extraordinary, the handling, and ſmelling bee's wax, is accompanied with ſenſations of the ſame tendency. Her ſon, a ſtrong, healthy young man, labours under nearly a ſimilar diſpoſition.

* *Qui mel, in Heraclea Ponti naſcens, ederunt, aut biberunt, iis eadem accidunt quæ ab aconito ſumpto ingruunt.* P. ÆGINET. lib. V c. 57.

I have

I have long thought that many children are loſt, from inattention; or, more properly ſpeaking, from not knowing the peculiarities, by which temperaments wonderfully differ.

The phyſical antipathies of children are never looked for; and never diſcovered.

How many infants linger in a painful manner, and periſh by convulſions, where no cauſe is known, or ſuſpected!

Sudden illneſs not to be defined,—and ſudden death, without any previous indiſpoſition, or traceable veſtiges on diſſection after death,—are ſubjects on which little has been ſaid, and nothing done.

Averſion from things obnoxious to phyſical organization, and repugnance to receive whatever diſturbs the functions connected by ſympathy, are obſervable in all animals.

But this ſpontaneous reſiſtance of nature is always overpowered in children; and is confounded with that indiſcriminate deſire or diſguſt, which perhaps would often fatally miſguide them.

In advanced age, antipathies demonſtrate themſelves; and frequently in the moſt irreſiſtible, and diſtreſſing manner.

Rhu-

Rhubarb, among ſeveral articles which might be mentioned, violently diſorders ſome people, of all characters of habit, and periods of life. And yet this drug is forced down the throat of every infant, the moment it comes into the world.

Oil acts as a poiſon to ſome people; but, as it does not poiſon every body, it is adminiſtered to infants, without ſuſpicion.

Even manna ſometimes acts as a poiſon.

My motives here, are not to enumerate the dangerous conſequences, and ſolitary inſtances of ſingular antipathy: otherwiſe, charges might be brought againſt every article, conſtituting our daily food.

Bacon ſays, " all life hath a ſympathy with *ſalt* * " This is true; and the ſame may be ſaid of ſugar. I have one inſtance of antipathy on record, however, againſt ſalt †; I know of none againſt ſugar. But doubtleſs there are inſtances, where individuals diſlike ſugar: but I never knew an inſtance of ſugar diſagreeing with any perſon.

This ſubject leads to an extenſive field, which has ſcarcely been entered, except by

* Hiſt. Nat. cent 10. art. 982.

† Bartholom. à Maranta. *Method. Cogn. Simpl. Med. lib.* 3. *cap.* 13.

thoſe

thofe who have had no defire to apply the culture of it to good and rational purpofes.

I fhould proceed further; but I have faid enough: as my object here is chiefly to recommend attention to fuch as have the care of the diet, and regimen of children; that they may keep a jealous eye on the operations of any article of food, or medicine, which has been known to produce injurious effects in habits, under the influence of Idiocracy.

Aged people, who have no teeth, and whofe digeftive faculties are impaired, and as incapable as thofe of infants, may like infants live on fugar.

I could produce many inftances where aged people have been fupported many years, by fcarcely any thing but fugar.

Taken in tea, milk, and beer, it has been found not only fufficient to fuftain nature, but has caufed lean people to grow fat, and has increafed the vigour of their bodies. The late king of Sardinia ate a great quantity of fugar daily. He ate it by itfelf; without diffolving it, or mixing it with any thing. It was his chief

chief food. After his death, his body was opened, and all his viſcera were perfectly ſound.

The great duke of *Beaufort*, as he was called, who died about an hundred years ago at the age of ſeventy, was opened; his viſcera were found in the ſame manner; as perfect as in a perſon of twenty: with his teeth white, and firm. He had for forty years before his death uſed a pound of ſugar daily, in his wine, chocolate, and ſweet-meats.

SLARE ſays, "his grandfather Mr. *Malory* was ſtrong and chearful in his eighty-ſecond year; at which time his hair changed ſomewhat dark; his old teeth came out, puſhed away by young ones; which continued ſo to do until he had a new ſet of teeth complete. He lived eaſy, and free from pain, or ſickneſs, until his hundredth year, when he died. He uſed ſugar to a great degree in all his food, vegetable, and animal; and delighted in all manner of ſweet-meats."

He ſays, "he followed the practice of his grandfather; and uſed ſugar in every thing he ate and drank: and in the ſixty-ſeventh year of his age all his teeth were ſound, and firm, and in their full number."

I know

I know a perſon at this time, about eighty years old, who has lived for ſeveral years almoſt on ſugar; and is as healthy and ſtrong, and as youthful in appearance, as moſt people at fifty.

The cauſe of this fondneſs for ſugar, was a paralytic affection, with which ſhe was attacked nearly twenty years ago, which prevented her, for a conſiderable time, ſwallowing any thing but fluids, in which a portion of ſugar was diſſolved.

Her diet now conſiſts of ſugar, and the ſimple vehicles in which it is taken; theſe are tea, milk, gruel, barley water, roaſted and boiled apples; and beer, generally for ſupper.

Animal food is not neceſſary for the pleaſurable exiſtence, and bodily health of man *; for mental pleaſure and health, perhaps, quite the contrary.

Yet the ſtreets of London ſeem to oppoſe theſe facts, with proofs ſhocking to reflecting minds. Blood flows in almoſt every gutter. In the very central, and moſt frequented places in the town,—what an horrid picture do the ſlaughter-

* *Prodiga divitias alimentaque mitia tellus*
Suggerit; atque epulas ſine cæde et ſanguine præbet.

OVID *Met. L. XV. v* 81, 82.

ſlaughter-houſes preſent!—The ſight of expiring and agoniſed animals, tumbled in heaps, while other poor trembling victims are gazing on, indicating by their appearance, their ſenſibility and ſufferings, and the knowledge of their approaching fate.

This practice in the public ſtreets, and markets, is not leſs diſgraceful to humanity, than to decency; and ought to be ſuppreſſed. The people's eyes are defiled with ſavage impreſſions; and their ideas rendered impure and brutal.—Their hearts, hardened by ſuch cruel ſcenes, are incapable of moral or ſocial virtue.—" Damned cuſtom" has

" ———————————— braz'd them ſo,
" That they are proof and bulwark againſt ſenſe *."

In the time of PYTHAGORAS †, ſugar was unknown; even to this great traveller. Otherwiſe his philoſophy would have had more converts. His diet was impracticable in moſt countries, from bulk, carriage, and ſeaſon. There is more nouriſhment in a pound of ſugar, than in a load of pulſe, or vegetables.

* *Hamlet.*

† 500 years before the Chriſtian æra.

If

If the pure, the divine PYTHAGORAS, undergoing the changes he ſuggeſted *, be now in this our planet, and conſcious of his former being, how muſt his holy ſpirit be depreſſed at the diſappointment of the flattering hope he once had formed; that mankind would riſe on his foundation, to the heights of truth; by living according to the ſimplicity of nature, and the dictates of reaſon; that their brutal hunt after the lives of God's creatures, and making a ſcience of butchery, would ſtop; and that the earth would ceaſe to repreſent a grazing ground, for ſlaughter; and its bloody inhabitants a maſs of canibals!

Two centuries have not elapſed, ſince it can be properly ſaid, that ſugar has become an ingredient in the popular diet of Europe.

There is now ſcarcely any perſon who does not mix, more or leſs of it, in his daily food; excepting the poor, remote inhabitants of the interior, and northern parts of Europe; whoſe cold, watery diet, moſt requires it.

* *Spiritus, eque feris humana in corpora tranſit,*
Inque feras noſter; nec tempore deperit ullo.
OVID. *Met. l. XV. v.* 167, 168.

The increaſed conſumption of ſugar, and the increaſing demand for it, exceed all compariſon with any other article, uſed as an auxiliary, in food: for, ſuch is the influence of ſugar, that once touching the nerves of taſte, no perſon was ever known to have the power of relinquiſhing the deſire for it.

When ſugar was firſt introduced into England, it is difficult to aſcertain; CHAUCER, in his Troilus and Creſſida, written in 1380, mentions, allegorically, the ſweetneſs of ſugar*; and, though it was in uſe in 1466, yet, until it was brought from the Brazils, about 1580, to Portugal, and imported from thence, it was chiefly confined to feaſts, and to medicine.

The quantity conſumed in England has always kept increaſing; though the whole conſumption for nearly a century, ſubſequent to this period, was inconſiderable.

The importation of ſugar into England in 1700 amounted to 481,425 hundred weight; or 48,142 hogſheads, at ten hundred weight each. The price then was thirty-two ſhillings the hundred weight.

* "So let your daungir *ſugrid* ben alite." Lib. II. l. 384.

The

The importation into England and Scotland on an average, for 1787, 1788, 1789, and 1790, amounted annually to 1,952,262 hundred weight.

The annual exportation during this period was, on an average, 296,996 hundred weight; which leaves the annual consumption in England and Scotland 1,655,266 hundred weight; or 118,233 hogsheads, of fourteen hundred weight each *.

Thus we find 185,389,792 pounds of sugar are annually consumed in England and Scotland.

But the proportion consumed in Scotland is small; not exceeding 12,000 hogsheads, or 18,816,448 pounds. The consumption then in England only, is 166,573,344 pounds.

Now taking the population of England at 8,000,000, the proportion of sugar to each individual, if each individual had his share, would be about twenty pounds per annum.

These calculations are made, reducing the whole to *raw*, or *muscovado* sugar.

The consumption in Ireland is not in this calculation. Ireland consumes 20,000 hogsheads per annum,

* From 1772 to 1775 the average consumption was 114,613½ hogsheads *per annum*.

Sugar is not an article of ſmuggling; and there were no prize-ſugars at the above period.

Before the Furies lighted their torches in St. *Domingue*, that beautiful iſland yielded, for the benefit of mankind, 200,000 hogſheads of ſugar.

The importation then, into all Europe, from every part of the world, was about 500,000 hogſheads.

The Eaſt Indies have not given us a quantity exceeding 5,000 hogſheads per annum. The Eaſt Indies cannot, I believe, ſpare much more for the Engliſh market, without further expenſive arrangements.

If Jamaica, and the other Engliſh ſugar iſlands, were to ſhare the fate of St. *Domingue*, by the horrors of war, a diſtreſs would ariſe, not only in England, but in Europe, not confined to the preſent generation, but that would deſcend to the child unborn.—Of ſuch importance has the agriculture of half a million of Africans *, become to Europeans.

* The negroes employed in the Weſt Indies, in cultivating the cane, and manufacturing ſugar, do not much exceed this number. Altogether there are, in the Engliſh colonies about 461,684 blacks; and in the French colonies about 489,265. In Jamaica, in the year 1698, there were 40,000 blacks, and 7,365 whites. In 1741, 100,000 blacks, and 10,000 whites. In 1787, 255,780 blacks, and 23,000 whites. The population in that iſland, at this time, is about the ſame.

The

The loſs of ſugar cannot be eſtimated, by a ſurvey of the diet of Europe, before ſugar was known. If it were poſſible that people could retrograde into the habits of that time, they would want ſome of the means then in uſe for their ſupport.

From the loſs of ſugar, many articles and vegetable mixtures, which now conſtitute the moſt agreeable and moſt wholeſome parts of the food, particularly of youth and delicate people, would be uſeleſs; and for which we have no ſalutary ſubſtitute.

There are ſome ſaccharite enthuſiaſts who attribute to the uſe of ſugar the extinction of the plague in Europe;—that is not the caſe:—but it has certainly contributed to ſuppreſs the native malady of England—the *Scurvy*.

That ſtate of the habit which we denominate ſcurvy, perhaps the parent of ſcrophula and conſumption, diſpoſes the ſyſtem to the ravages of fevers; and hence the great mortality in former times; when peſtilential fevers and plagues invaded the Engliſh, deeply infected by the ſcurvy.

An article in conſtant uſe, to the extent ſugar now is, muſt have conſiderable influence in diſpoſing the body to receive or reſiſt diſeaſe. Becauſe the blood, and the growth, or changes, and ſupport of the frame, depend on the aliment received into the ſtomach; and the general ſtate of the ſyſtem, excluſive of climate and particular organization, muſt be affected accordingly.

The formation of the body, and more of the inclination of the mind than is generally imagined, depend on the nature and quality of our food. This I had occaſion formerly to remark *.

Without reſorting to the metamorphoſis of *Nebuchadnezzar*, MONTESQUIEU was ſo perſuaded of this doctrine, that he aſſerts in many animals, excepting their mere bones, their mental as well as their corporal character, is decided by it.

This is indeed ſo ſtrongly diſtinguiſhable among the lower claſſes, in ſome countries, that one would almoſt conclude, a man is but a walking vegetable—or an hieroglyphic—importing the food, of which he is compounded.

The ſavageneſs of the wildeſt animals is ſoftened by diet; and it ſometimes appears as if ferocity would ſleep quietly in the frame, unleſs awakened by ſenſations excited by the colour, ſcent, and taſte of blood.

* Treatiſe on COFFEE, Ed. 5. page 1.

I knew a perſon at Kingſton, in Jamaica, a Mr. *Benjamin Parker*, who had nearly loſt his life, by an event which illuſtrates this ſuppoſition.

He had a Spaniſh-main tyger, which he brought up on milk and ſugar, and bread,—from the time it was newly born, until it was nearly full grown. It ſlept in his room, frequently on his bed, and went about the houſe like a ſpaniel. He was taken ill of a fever. I directed him to be bled. Soon after the operation he fell aſleep, with the tyger by his ſide, on the bed. During his ſleeping, the arm bled conſiderably. The tyger, which as yet had never ſeen blood, or taſted animal food, while Mr. *Parker* was ſleeping, had gnawed his ſhirt ſleeve, and the bloody part of the ſheet into a thouſand pieces. He had alſo detached the compreſs, and got at the bleeding orifice of the vein, and licked up the blood running from it. The impatient animal, forgetting in a moment his domeſtic education, and the kindneſs of his maſter, began to uſe the arm with ſome roughneſs with his teeth, which awaked Mr. *Parker*. On his riſing up in his bed, the tyger and maſter were in mutual conſternation. The tyger gave a ſpring, and jumped on an high cheſt of drawers in the room; from that, to the chairs, and tables, and ran about the houſe in wild and horrible phrenzy I arrived at the houſe at the time of this confuſion. The tyger eſcaped into the garden:—where he was ſhot.

Europe is in a much better ſtate of bodily health than it was formerly. It has alſo undergone great changes in its mental condition; as all Europe feels. There is ſtill ſome room for improvement in both. But the latter is a devious road from my object, which I muſt leave to divines and politicians; and confine myſelf to a path, with which I hope I am better acquainted—WARWICK LANE.

There are no diſtempers now in Europe maiming and rotting whole countries;—and, I conceive, what our anceſtors reprobated, and dreaded the importation of ſo much, under the appellation of luxuries, has had a conſiderable ſhare in this alteration.

Since European countries have had intercourſe with the Eaſt and Weſt Indies, and a free and enlarged traffic with each other, and commerce has ſupplied the deficiences of one country, from the ſuperfluities of another, Europe has greatly improved in its regimen.

The popular diet before was crude, coarſe, and unwholeſome. A royal Engliſh dinner of the

the twelfth century would be despised by a modern tradesman. Spices, wine, sugar, and culinary chemistry, made no part of the repast.

But people have not used these bounties of nature, and art, with prudence. If they have now no dread of some of the heavy calamities which then made their ravaging visitations, there are too many who have by their excesses acquired others, which embitter the chronical hours of declining life.

This reflexion does not extend to labouring people; they are strangers to more of foreign productions than what barely qualify their food for health; and though short-lived, they are providentially secured against the miseries of ill-used opulence,—the derangements of gluttony and repletion: the principal diseases in England.—Old CORNARO's bodily doctrines for health and longevity *, are as repugnant to the English, as LUTHER's spiritual doctrines were to him.

Diseases in general would be uniform, and never undergo much alteration, were people

* *Tale si partisse da tavola, che potesse ancora mangiare, & bere.* Discorsi della Vita Sobria. Anno 1620.

to feed only on the produce of their own ſoil. This appears in the diſeaſes of cattle; and alſo in thoſe of Indians; and people living in a ſtate of nature, without foreign communication: and this likewiſe appears, in a great degree, among artificers and manufacturers, and ſuch as cannot deviate in habit.

In commercial countries, where articles of foreign growth, and diſſimilar climates enter into dietetic uſe, with the generality of a people, it is impoſſible that the type of their diſeaſes ſhould remain ſtationary; or that ſome will not appear, and others diſappear, from any conſiderable change, or ſubverſion of cuſtom.

Within my memory the inflammatory tendency of diſeaſes in Europe, has gradually diminiſhed. There are not ſo many pleureſies among the reapers in harveſt, as there were formerly.

Every phyſician knows, that the practice employed in fevers in the laſt century is now obſolete; and that the practice of the preceding century is ſtill more ſo. I ſpeak alſo of diſeaſes in general. Accurate phyſicians know, that fevers are continually diſappointing them.

The

The ſcience of medicine therefore has not improved,—it has changed: becauſe diſeaſes change. It is to be remembered, that HIPPOCRATES, CELSUS, and GALEN, knew all that was poſſible to be known in their time; yet we cannot go by their writings; and, if they had left us nothing but their preſcriptions, we ſhould not now be much benefited in our practice, by their labours.

I ſhall now conclude this treatiſe; not without hopes that the difficulties I mentioned, in the way of a correct hiſtory of SUGAR, have ſufficiently appeared, to juſtify my motives in premiſing them: and to extenuate many defects in the execution of this undertaking.

The political government, civil adminiſtration of public and private affairs, and the commercial intereſts of the ſugar colonial ſettlements, have been well delineated by hiſtorians of different nations.

In England, we have the father of correct Engliſh-Weſt-Indian literature, Mr. EDWARD LONG; and, ſince his invaluable publication, we have the learned, and comprehenſive view of thoſe countries by Mr. BRYAN EDWARDS.

Theſe

Theſe enlightened hiſtorians have left ſcarcely any information unfolded, reſpecting the Weſt-Indian iſlands, from the time they were firſt known to Europeans, down to their own days.

Much alſo of curious matter has been given by other ingenious men, concerning branches of the natural hiſtory of the Weſt-Indies; but the anatomy in general, in this department, is without their method and ſcience.

Great beauties, and ſublime objects, are ſtill untouched by Europeans; and the SUGAR CANE, the heart of the ſolar world, has never been diſſected.

By the Planter, the SUGAR CANE has been no further conſidered, than as it relates to the engine, and the copper.

In the precious fluid of its cells, he has found that, which philoſophers have ſo long ſearched for in vain.

Wrapt in the rich fancy of its all-powerful influence, his chief concern is in its tranſmutation:—but he gives the world the bleſſings of his alchemy.

In the ſeaſon of this great—this faſcinating work,—a ſugar-plantation repreſents the days of Saturn—Every animal ſeems to be a member of the golden age.

At

At home, the merchant, from this tranſatlantic operation, ſupports legions of manufacturers. With pointed finger on the globe, he follows the car of phœbus with anxious care, through the heavenly ſigns propitious to his views; collects his rays from equatorial climes; diffuſes their genial warmth over the frigid regions of the earth, and makes the induſtrious world one great family.

AN ACCOUNT of the QUANTITY of BRITISH PLANTATION SUGAR ANNUALLY IMPORTED INTO GREAT BRITAIN; with the amount of duties paid thereon, from the year 1764 to 1791, both inclusive. Also, an ACCOUNT of the QUANTITY of RAW and REFINED SUGARS EXPORTED FROM GREAT BRITAIN in the above periods; with the amount of Drawbacks and Bounties paid thereon, distinguishing each year, and the Raw from the Refined; distinguishing also the quantities exported to Ireland.

	British Plantation Sugar imported.						British Plantation Sugar exported.												Refined Sugar exported.											
Yrs.	Quantity.			Duty.			To Ireland.			To other Parts.			Total.			Drawbacks.			To Ireland.			To all other Parts.			Total.			Bounties.		
	Cwt.	q.	lb.	L.	s.	d.	Cwt.	q.	lb.	Cwt.	q.	lb.	Cwt.	q.	lb.	L.	s.	d.	Cwt.	q	lb.	Cwt.	q.	lb.	Cwt.	q.	lb.	L.	s.	d.
1764	1,488,079	–	11	467,814	17	4	119,670	1	13	77,908	3	12	197,579	–	25	62,734	8	2	3,630	–	2	172,672	3	21	176,302	3	23	127,819	11	10
5	1,227,159	3	18	385,788	7	–	136,004	3	8	13,120	1	25	149,125	1	5	47,160	17	3	9,771	1	12	105,074	–	16	114,851	2	–	83,269	6	9
6	1,522,732	2	10	478,709	1	–	125,558	1	26	3,678	–	6	129,236	2	4	40,871	–	6	5,378	–	14	22,223	3	24	27,602	–	10	2[illegible],011	10	3
7	1,538,834	1	8	480,895	19	9	180,156	2	20	29,376	3	5	209,533	1	25	66,264	19	–	5,584	–	13	30,384	–	27	35,968	1	12	26,077	1	2
8	1,651,512	2	14	519,194	5	6	183,049	3	5	44,144	–	16	227,193	3	21	71,850	1	8	6,552	–	6	32,721	2	21	39,273	2	27	28,473	8	5½
9	1,525,070	–	5	479,443	17	–	195,382	3	5	21,001	–	23	216,384	–	–	68,431	8	9	7,414	1	15	26,627	1	1	34,041	2	16	24,680	3	3¾
1770	1,818,229	1	23	571,605	17	5	127,181	2	–	72,566	3	9	199,738	1	9	63,167	4	9	3,802	3	6	39,806	1	13	43,609	1	19	31,616	16	8¾
1	1,492,096	2	24	469,077	17	10	192,120	2	17	3,738	2	12	195,859	1	1	61,940	9	10	8,842	3	20	46,367	–	22	55,210	–	13	40,027	6	9½
2	1,829,721	–	8	575,218	10	4	172,269	2	5	11,596	–	3	183,865	2	8	58,128	6	7	10,167	3	2	21,813	–	17	31,980	3	19	23,186	3	3¾
3	1,804,080	2	26	565,157	17	6	184,252	2	17	4,937	–	22	189,189	3	11	59,831	5	8	9,784	–	27	19,050	3	15	28,835	–	13	20,905	9	3¾
4	2,029,725	1	25	638,104	18	8	211,304	1	25	13,637	2	10	224,942	–	7	71,137	18	3	7,899	2	14	24,613	3	9	32,513	1	22	23,572	5	2
5	2,021,059	3	23	635,370	14	1	255,684	3	12	82,963	1	17	344,648	1	1	108,995	–	2	9,972	3	3	59,767	1	3	69,740	–	6	50,561	19	9¼
6	1,726,507	1	16	542,770	15	–	201,757	–	7	113,696	1	8	315,453	1	15	99,763	14	11	12,941	2	3	55,907	2	9	68,849	–	12	49,915	12	–
7	1,416,291	1	5	445,246	11	4	150,241	3	–	11,572	3	26	161,814	2	26	51,173	18	2	15,530	2	21	55,522	2	21	71,053	1	14	51,513	13	11¼
8	1,521,457	1	24	478,304	13	7	130,865	1	26	11,897	2	19	142,763	–	17	45,148	16	10	7,013	1	8	48,908	–	17	55,921	1	25	40,543	1	4¾
9	1,525,833	–	—	506,671	18	5	92,793	1	25	6,223	2	16	99,017	–	13	32,870	10	6	7,411	1	3	18,716	1	18	26,127	2	21	18,942	11	5¾
1780	1,394,559	1	23	463,080	19	–	116,700	–	19	1,853	2	6	118,553	2	25	39,391	18	–	16,254	2	7	22,068	1	18	38,322	3	25	27,784	3	1½
1	1,080,848	2	9	633,647	2	–	142,493	1	24	27,067	1	3	169,560	2	27	99,228	7	3	12,033	2	17	51,508	1	12	63,542	–	1	46,067	19	1½
2	1,374,269	3	24	844,030	15	10	83,646	–	11	7,615	1	21	91,261	2	4	56,049	15	8	7,643	–	22	24,824	1	12	32,467	2	6	42,207	16	4¾
3	1,584,275	–	18	973,909	–	–	154,756	1	6	18,382	–	15	173,138	1	21	106,333	17	11	10,977	–	24	93,798	–	9	104,775	1	5	136,207	17	7¾
4	1,782,386	–	3	1,094,082	1	7	133,149	1	19	7,330	1	13	140,479	3	4	86,345	3	4	5,288	–	27	126,321	–	27	131,609	1	20	171,092	6	6¼
5	2,075,909	3	24	1,274,954	14	2	199,218	2	24	3,735	1	9	202,954	–	5	125,154	19	9	6,894	1	5	129,099	1	21	135,993	2	26	176,791	17	–¼
6	1,613,965	1	14	992,301	–	–	98,266	–	5	3,767	2	2	102,033	2	7	62,665	11	2	8,700	3	17	73,049	3	12	81,750	3	1	106,275	19	8¾
7	1,926,621	–	26	1,188,083	1	10	196,636	3	20	2,779	1	16	199,416	1	8	122,973	7	11	14,320	1	4	62,415	–	15	76,735	1	19	99,756	–	10¾
8	2,065,817	1	23	1,273,920	15	–	138,681	3	19	6,391	2	10	145,073	2	1	89,461	19	10	8,001	2	22	77,399	2	21	85,401	1	15	111,021	15	11¾
9	1,936,440	–	2	1,194,915	2	6	148,245	3	–	5,561	2	15	153,813	1	15	99,808	19	11	10,702	1	11	127,837	2	–	138,539	3	11	180,101	16	–½
1790	1,882,106	–	4	1,160,645	12	4	139,193	3	24	2,991	1	7	142,185	1	3	87,680	18	4	8,484	–	–	111,332	2	10	119,817	–	4	155,762	2	11
1	1,808,950	–	7	1,350,893	10	9	123,086	3	22	12,383	3	14	135,470	3	8	81,116	11	1	10,626	–	16	147,947	2	8	158,573	3	24	206,146	3	–¾

The value of the whole of the Britifh Weft Indian products imported, for the following years, according to the Cuftom-Houfe prices.

Years.	Value.	Years.	Value.
	£.		£.
1764	2,391,552	1778	3,059,922
1765	2,196,549	1779	2,836,489
1766	2,704,114	1780	2,612,236
1767	2,690,673	1781	2,023,546
1768	2,942,717	1782	2,612,910
1769	2,686,714	1783	2,820,387
1770	2,110,026*	1784	3,531,705
1771	2,979,378†	1785	4,400,956
1772	3,530,082	1786	3,484,025
1773	2,902,407	1787	3,758,087
1774	3,574,702	1788	4,307,866
1775	3,688,795	1789	3,917,301
1776	3,340,949	1790	3,854,204
1777	2,840,802		

* The value of the produce of St. *Domingue*, according to an account publifhed in France this year, amounted to £.2,923,333; viz. Sugar £.2,400,000; Coffee £.83,333; Cotton £.120,000; Indigo £.300,000; Tanned Leather £.20,000.

† The accounts preceding, refer to England only. Thofe for the year 1771, and all fubfequent, are for England and Scotland.

N.B. The total of fhips cleared outwards from England and Scotland, from December 1786 to December 1787, was 528, amounting to 123,581 tons; and the total of thofe entered inwards was 576, amounting to 132,222 tons. The value of goods, Britifh produce, and manufactures, exported from Great Britain to the Weft Indian colonies in 1787, was £.1,463,879. 14*s*. 11*d*.

An

An account of the products entered for exportation from St. Domingue to France, for the following years.

Years.	Sugar Clayed.	Ditto Mufcovado	Coffee.	Cotton.	Indigo.
	lb.	lb.	lb.	lb.	lb.
1783	77,339,113	44,312,919	44,573,479	4,871,718	1,868,728
1784	65,053,050	77,344,464	52,885,095	4.756,857	1,555,142
1785	66,589,357	83,610,521	51,368,109	4,486,261	1,546,575
1786	71,063,697	61,887,814	52,180,311	5,203,161	1,103,907
1787	56,182,403	72,896,676	70,003,161	6,806,174	1,166,177
1788	70,227,709	93,177,512	68,151,181	6,286,126	930,016
1789	47,516,531	91,899,963	76,286,530	6,871,204	958,626

N. B. The above are heavier than Englifh weights by 8 per cent.

St. *Domingue* was generally confidered in France to yield about two-thirds of all their Weft Indian produce; and, in 1788, this ifland alone loaded for France 580 fhips, of 370¾ tons on a medium, and 110 of 740 tons: exclufive of the numerous French and foreign veffels employed in the trade with North and South America, amounting, in the whole, to 296,435 tons, nearly equal to one-third of the private fhips of Great Britain.

FINIS.

MISCELLANEOUS MEDICAL OBSERVATIONS.

MEDICAL OBSERVATIONS.

COW-POX.

THE *Cow-Pox* has lately appeared in England. This is a new ſtar in the Æſculapian ſyſtem. It was firſt obſerved from the Provinces. It is ſo luminous there, that the greaſy-heeled hind feet of Pegaſus are viſible to the naked eye; the hidden parts of that conſtellation, which have puzzled aſtronomers, as to the ſex of Pegaſus; and which HIPPARCHUS, TYCHO, HEVELIUS, FLAMSFEAD, and HERSCHEL, could never diſcover. The reaſon now is evident.

The medical Pythoniſſas are divided in their opinion reſpecting this phenomenon.

Great events are foreboded.—Some pretend that a reſtive greaſy-heeled horſe will kick down all the old gally-pots of GALEN.—Others, that the people of England are becoming like the inhabitants of a wilderneſs, beyond the land of Cathay, ſeen in 1333, by the rare and inimitable Sir JOHN MANDEVILE,—who, he ſays, were "wild, with horns on their heads, very hideous and ſpeak not; but rout as ſwine *."

To preſerve, as far as in me lies, the geneſis of this deſirable—this excelling diſtemper, to poſterity,—I mention, that it is ſaid to originate in what is called, the *greaſy heel* diſtemper, in horſes. Theſe *greaſy heels*, are ſaid to infect the hands of people who dreſs and clean them. The hands of people thus infected, are ſaid to infect the teats of cows in milking them. The teats of theſe infected cows in return, are ſaid to infect the hands of others who milk them; and ſo the diſtemper, is ſaid to be propagated among the country people.

The virtues of this charming diſtemper, are ſaid to be an amulet againſt the ſmall-pox; that it is mild and innocent; and communicated with ſafety by inoculation.

Wonderful things do certainly appear in all ages; the great ERASMUS mentions a man, one *Philario*, an Italian, who in Holland was very much afflicted with worms. While the worms

* Quarto ed. 1677. chap. 87.

were

were in his body, he ſpoke the Dutch language fluently. When his phyſician cured him of the diſorder, he could not ſpeak a word of that language. The Dutch worms and the Dutch language left *Philario* together * !

In this *Cowmania*, it is not enough for reaſon to concede, that the Cow-pox may leſſen, *for a time*, the diſpoſition in the habit to receive the infection of the *Small-pox*.

All cutaneous determinations ; catarrhal fevers ; and every diſeaſe of the lymphatics ; and medicine, tending, to what SYDENHAM would call depurating that ſyſtem, do the ſame.

Surgeons know, that the firſt inflammation of any membrane is the moſt violent : and that reiterated inflammation deadens ſenſibility.

But no complaint to which people are repeatedly ſubject, as the Cow-pox, can perform all circumſtances in the habit, equivalent to the Small-pox, which people never have but once.

Beſides, the Small-pox does not deſtroy the diſpoſition in the habit to receive the Cow-pox.

* *Crede quod habes, et habes*—ERASME !

If that be the caſe, the Small-pox and the Cow-pox, then, are not analogous ; but radically diſſimilar.

The Small-pox is undoubtedly an evil ; but we underſtand the extent of that ill ; which we had better bear,

" than fly to others that we know not of."

Inoculation has diſarmed the Small-pox of its terrors ; and reduced it to management *.

I have inoculated in the Weſt Indies, and in Europe, ſeveral thouſands. I never loſt a patient. I ſpeak ſubject to the animadverſions of contemporaries. I ſhould not have mentioned this, but that it gives me an opportunity of ſaying many others, whom I know, have done the ſame, with the ſame ſucceſs. Accidents, in the inoculated Small-pox, are uncommon ; and we all know from experience, that diſeaſe, properly treated, leaves nothing after it injurious to the conſtitution.

The ſubject, reſpecting the diſtempers of the brute creation, of which we know but little, has not been overlooked by the learned and

* In 1721, and the two following years, there were only 447 perſons inoculated in Great Britain.

curious ;

curious; nor is hiſtory deſtitute of many inſtances of their fatal effects to the human race *.

Can any perſon ſay what may be the conſequences of introducing the *Lues Bovilla*, a *beſtial* humour—into the human frame, after a long lapſe of years?

Who knows, beſides, what ideas may riſe, in the courſe of time, from a *brutal* fever having excited its incongruous impreſſions on the brain?

Who knows, alſo, but that the human character may undergo ſtrange mutations from *quadrupedan* ſympathy; and that ſome modern Paſiphaë may rival the fables of old?

I mention this ſerious trifling, not from diſreſpect to the ingenious, nor to diſcourage inquiry; the object well deſerves it;—but the doctrine of engrafting diſtempers is not yet comprehended by the wiſeſt men: and I wiſh to arreſt the hurry of public credulity, until

* LUES BOVILLA, *Thierſcuchen Giſt*,—"Homines interdum ſub incauta pecorum ægrotantium medicatione, vel a detractione pellis mortuorum, imo etiam coriarios alutam e pellibus demortuorum animalium fabricantes inficit, & febrem putrido-inflammatóriam cum bullis ichoroſis, aut papulis nigris, partem cui incident, valde inflammantibus excitat." PLENCK. *Toxicolog.* p. 60. Ed. Viennæ, 1785.

the ſubject has undergone a deep, calm, and diſpaſſionate ſcrutiny; and to guard parents againſt ſuffering their children becoming victims to experiment.

What miſery may be brought on a family after many years of imaginary ſecurity!

The Yaws.

There are ſeveral diſtempers of *beſtial* origin, I have no doubt.

The *Yaws* is one of them; and, not being underſtood in Europe, and a well-known affliction in the ſugar colonies, it is not foreign to my purpoſe to notice it here.

The *yaws* naturally is an original African diſtemper. It may be communicated to white people, as it is to blacks, by inoculation, and by accidental contact, when the ulcerous matter is carried into the habit by abſorption, as it is called. I have ſeen ſeveral ſhocking inſtances of this ſort. But it breaks out in negroes without any communication, ſociety, or contact.

The ſeeds of the *yaws* deſcend from thoſe who have ever had it, to their lateſt poſterity.

No

No period from infàncy to age exempts them from it. Its appearance is uncertain.

CHEVALIER and HILLARY ſpeak of the *yaws*; but their accounts are erroneous. CHEVALIER perhaps never ſew it*. HILLARY often ſaw it; but he miſunderſtands HALI ABBAS, whom he has quoted; endeavouring to prove it is common in Arabia as well as in Africa†.

TURNER never ſaw it, and is abſurd‡; and our great SYDENHAM, who was a total ſtranger to it, ſcarcely ever committed an error, but in this inſtance §.

The *yaws* differs altogether from every other diſorder, in its origin, progreſs, and termination.

Left to itſelf, it ſometimes departs in 9, 12, 15, or 18 months, without leaving behind it any inconveniency. Sometimes it remains much longer, and ends in ſhocking nodes, and diſtortions of the bones. Many are deſtroyed by it. No perſon is ſubject to it twice.

From want of care and proper management, the torments of the *yaws* ſurpaſs all deſcrip-

* *Maladies de St Domingue.* 1752.

† Diſeaſes of *Barbadoes*, 1759.

‡ *Syphilis.* p 6. ed. 5.

§ *Opera Univerſa*, p. 327, ed. *Lugd. Batav.* 1741. N. B. written *anno* 1679.

tion,

tion, from the *bone ache*, and dreadful agonizing curvatures, and caries of the legs, arms, collar-bones, wriſts, and almoſt every other bone, and articulation in the body.

There is alſo, ſometimes, a relic after the original malady is gone, called the *maſter yaw*; this is an inveterate ulcer, proceeding from the largeſt *yaw*, or chief determination of the eruption.

Generally, this diſtemper terminates in what are called *crab yaws*. Theſe are painful ſores, or cracks in the feet, ſometimes ſpongy, ſometimes hard and callous.

There are two ſorts of *yaws*, like the two ſpecies of *Farcy* in horſes; the *common yaws* and the *running yaws*.

The *common yaws*, without fever or indiſpoſition, begins with ſmall pimples, which ſoon increaſe, and appear in round, white, flabby, eruptions, from about the ſize of a pea to that of a large ſtrawberry, ſeparately, or in cluſters, in different parts of the body. Theſe eruptions do not appear all at once; and, when ſome are declining, and others diſappearing, a freſh crop comes out in a different part of the body. Sometimes a few doſes of ſulphur will force them out, when they are thought to be entirely gone from the habit.

The

The *running yaws* breaks out in ſpreading cutaneous ulcers, diſcharging a great quantity of acrid corroſive matter, in different parts of the body. This is the worſt ſort.

The cure of the *yaws* is now underſtood by ſkilful practitioners. Inoculation is performed with ſucceſs. Care ſoon removes the principal miſchief of the diſtemper; and the *crab yaws* are eaſily cured in the manner which I have related in another publication *.

Formerly there was no regular method of treating the *yaws* in the Weſt Indies. It was thought to be a diſorder that would have its courſe, and, if interrupted, that it would be dangerous.

It was then the cuſtom, when a negro was attacked with it, to ſeparate him from the reſt, and ſend him to ſome lonely place by the ſea ſide, to bathe; or into the mountains, to ſome Proviſion Ground, or Plantain Walk; where he could act as a watchman, and maintain himſelf, without any expence to the eſtate, until he was well: then he was brought back to the Sugar-Work.

But this rarely happened. A cold, damp, ſmoky hut, for his habitation; ſnakes and li-

* *Treatiſe on Tropical Diſeaſes,* Ed. 3, p. 519.

zards

zards his companions; crude, viſcid food, and bad water, his only ſupport; and ſhunned as a leper;—he uſually ſunk from the land of the living.

But ſome of theſe abandoned exiles lived, in ſpite of the common law of nature, and ſurvived a general mutation of their muſcles, ligaments, and oſteology; became alſo hideouſly white in their woolly hair and ſkin; with their noſes, like the beaks of old eagles—ſtarving the creatures, by obſtructing the paſſage to their mouths,—and their limbs and bodies twiſted and turned, by the force of the diſtemper, into ſhocking groteſque figures, reſembling woody excreſcences, or ſtumps of trees; or old Ægyptian figures, that ſeem as if they had been made of the ends of the human, and beginnings of the brutal form; which figures are, by ſome antiquaries, taken for gods, and by others, for devils.

In their baniſhment, their huts often became the receptacles of robbers and fugitive negroes; and, as they had no power to reſiſt any who choſe to take ſhelter in their hovels, had nothing to loſe, and were forſaken by the world, a tyger would hardly moleſt them. Their deſperate gueſts never did.

The

The hoſt of the hut, as he grew more miſ-ſhapen, generally became more ſubtile;—this we obſerve in England, in crooked ſcrophulous perſons;—as if Nature diſliked people's being both cunning, and ſtrong.

Many of their wayward viſitors were deeply ſkilled in magic, and what we call the *black art*, which they brought with them from Africa; and, in return for their accommodation, they uſually taught their landlord the myſteries of ſigils, ſpells, and ſorcery; and *illuminated* him in all the occult ſcience of Obi.

Theſe ugly, loathſome creatures thus became oracles of woods, and unfrequented places; and were reſorted to ſecretly, by the wretched in mind, and by the malicious, for wicked purpoſes.

Obi, and *gambling*, are the only inſtances I have been able to diſcover, among the natives of the negro land in Africa, in which any effort at combining ideas has ever been demonſtrated.

OBI.

The ſcience of Obi is very extenſive.

This Obi, or, as it is pronounced in the Engliſh Weſt Indies, *Obeah*, had its origin, like many cuſtoms among the Africans, from the ancient Ægyptians.

אוֹב *ōb* is a demon, a ſpirit of divination, and magic.

When Saul wanted to raiſe up Samuel from the dead, he ſaid to his ſervants, "Seek me a woman (בַּעֲלַת אוֹב *eminent for* ōb) that hath a familiar ſpirit."

His ſervants replied to him,

הִנֵּה אֵשֶׁת בַּעֲלַת אוֹב בְּעֵין דּוֹר

"*Behold there is a woman miſtreſs in the art of* ōb, *in Hen-dor.*"

When the witch of Hen-dor came to Saul, he ſaid to her,

קָסֳומִי נָא לִי בָּאוֹב

"*Divine, I pray thee, unto me, in thy witchcraft* ōb, and raiſe him up from the dead whom I ſhall name unto thee."

She

She accordingly raiſed up *Samuel*, from whom *Saul* had but an unpleaſant reception.

Saul muſt indeed have been "ſore diſtreſſed," to have recourſe to, and place his faith in, an art he perſecuted, and thought he had exterminated. For, during his reign,

הִכְרִית אֶת * הָאֹבוֹת וְאֶת † הַיִּדְּעֹנִי מִן הָאָרֶץ

"*He cut off magiciens, and foretellers of future events from the earth.* ‡"

Obi, for the purpoſes of bewitching people, or conſuming them by lingering illneſs, is made of grave dirt, hair, teeth of ſharks, and other animals, blood, feathers, egg-ſhells, images in wax, the hearts of birds, liver of mice §, and ſome potent roots, weeds, and buſhes, of which Europeans are at this time ignorant; but which were known, for the ſame purpoſes, to the ancients.

Certain mixtures of theſe ingredients are burnt; or buried very deep in the ground; or hung up a chimney; or on the ſide of an

* Εγγαστριμυθους. LXX. *Pythones*, Pagnin.

† Γνωστας. LXX. *Sciolum*, Pagnin.

‡ 1 *Samuel*, c. xxviii. v. 7, 8, and 9.

§ See *Iſaiah*, c. lxvi. v. 17. alſo, Pierius on the Ægyptian hieroglyphics.

 houſe;

houſe; or in a garden; or laid under the threſhold of the door of the party, to ſuffer; with incantation ſongs, or curſes, or ceremonies necromantically performed in planetary hours, or at midnight, regarding the aſpects of the moon. The perſon who wants to do the miſchief is alſo ſent to burying-grounds, or ſome ſecret place, where ſpirits are ſuppoſed to frequent, to invoke his, or her dead parents, or ſome dead friend, to aſſiſt in the curſe.

A negro, who thinks himſelf bewitched by OBI, will apply to an *Obi-man*, or *Obi-woman*, for cure.

Theſe magicians will interrogate the patient, as to the part of the body moſt afflicted. This part they will torture with pinching, drawing with gourds, or calabaſhes, beating, and preſſing. When the patient is nearly exhauſted with this rough *magnetiſing*, OBI brings out an old ruſty nail, or a piece of bone, or an aſs's tooth, or the jaw-bone of a rat, or a fragment of a quart-bottle, from the part; and the patient is well the next day.

The moſt wrinkled, and moſt deformed *Obian* magicians are moſt venerated. This was the caſe among the Ægyptians and Chaldeans.

In

In general, *Obi-men* are more ſagacious than *Obi-women*, in giving, or taking away diſeaſes; and in the application of poiſons. It is in their department to blind pigs, and poultry; and lame cattle.

In this ſurpriſing knowledge, the Africans are far ſuperior to the Indians, though they are alſo ſkilled in the veneſical art; and are matchleſs in arming their deadly arrows.

A negro *Obi-man* will adminiſter a baleful doſe from poiſonous herbs, and calculate its mortal effects to an hour, day, week, month, or year. Theſe maſters could inſtruct even Frier BACON; and frighten Thomas AQUINAS *.

It is the province of the *Obi-women* to diſpoſe of the paſſions. They ſell foul winds for inconſtant mariners †; dreams and phantaſies for jealouſy; vexation, and pains in the heart, for perfidious love; and for the perturbed, impatient, and wretched, at the tardy acts of time,—to turn in prophetic fury to a future page in the book of Fate,—and amaze the raviſhed ſenſe of the tempeſt-toſſed querent.

* The mechanical and magical ſkill of ROGER BACON has no parallel in hiſtory. He invented images that could ſpeak. THOMAS AQUINAS was ſo frightened at an automaton made by ALBERTUS MAGNUS, that he broke it in pieces.

† King *Ericus* of Sweedland had a cap, which by turning, he could make the wind blow from any quarter he pleaſed. OLAUS MAGNUS *de Gent. Sept.* lib. iii. c. 14.

The victims to this nefarious art, among the negroes in the West Indies, are more numerous than is generally known. No humanity of the master, nor skill in medicine, can relieve a negro, labouring under the influence of OBI. He will surely die; and of a disease that answers no description in nosology. This, when I first went to the colonies, perplexed me.

Laws have been made in the West Indies to punish this *Obian* practice with death; but they have been impotent and nugatory. Laws constructed in the West Indies, can never suppress the effect of ideas, the origin of which is in the centre of Africa.

There was a time, and that not very long ago, when poverty, uglinefs, and wrinkles, with palsied head and trembling limbs, constituted suspicions of OBI in England; and for which many old women have been tried, condemned, and hanged, as perpetrators of every untoward accident in their neighbourhood.

But the most bloody tragedy ever acted in the black theatre of superstition, was performed in New England, in North America, in 1692, by the hypochondriacal descendants of the moody melancholy English, who settled in that province.

Sir

Sir William Phipps was, at the breaking-out of this phrenzy, governor of the province. This governor was originally a ſhip-carpenter. He, in conjunction with a few wicked preachers, and magiſtrates, began ſuch a diabolical ſcene of murder, under the ſanction of legal forms, that went to exterminate every perſon who differed in opinion from, or was in any reſpect diſagreeable to, this inhuman gang, for witchcraft; the popular mental malady in that country. But the Governor was impeached for mal-adminiſtration, and ſuddenly removed from the province.

This horrid tranſaction was opened at *Salem*; where nineteen of the moſt pious and orderly inhabitants were hanged, and one was preſſed to death. An hundred more who were in priſon waiting for trial, and two hundred under accuſation eſcaped, by the Governor's removal.

The firſt victim in this horrid affair, was a Mr. *George Burroughs*, miniſter at *Falmouth*, a neighbouring village; a man of exemplary manners, and unblemiſhed character. After his execution he was dragged on the ground, by the halter with which he had been hanged, and thrown into a pit in a lonely wood, inhabited only by wild beaſts:—and, as a further mark of the brutality of theſe adminiſtrators of public affairs, his face, and one of his hands, were ordered to be left uncovered in the earth: which was accordingly done by the executioner.

Another irreproachable man, a Mr. *John Bradſtreet*, to ſave his life, fled from this juriſdiction. For wretches had been procured to ſwear, that Mr. *Bradſtreet* rode through the air on his dog, to witch meetings. The Governor and his party, loſing this intended victim, revenged themſelves on the dog; had him arreſted, and put to death, as an accomplice with his maſter.

This barbarous inſanity was called the *Witch Plague*. It was firſt ſet on foot by one *Parris*, miniſter of *Salem*. This fellow had a beautiful Indian maid, named *Tumba*, whom he had by ſome means or other procured from her native country, to attend upon his niece and daughter. Theſe girls, among many others, being attacked with nervous affections and the endemial deſpondency of that part of America, were deemed bewitched. In ſome of their diſtempered reveries, they fancied they had ſeen *Tumba's* ghoſt. Poor *Tumba* was ſeized; put into a dungeon in the common priſon; confeſſed herſelf a witch to ſave

her

her life: but her ruthlefs mafter, after beating her into the confeffion of what he wanted, and of which fhe was innocent, fold her to flavery to pay the gaoler's fees.

I faw the OBI of the famous negro robber, *Three fingered* JACK, the terror of Jamaica in 1780. The Maroons who flew him brought it to me *.

His OBI confifted of the end of a goat's horn, filled with a compound of grave dirt, afhes, the blood of a black cat, and human fat; all mixed into a kind of pafte. A cat's foot, a dried toad, a pig's tail, a flip of virginal parchment of kid's fkin, with characters marked in blood on it, were alfo in his *Obian* bag.

Thefe, with a keen fabre, and two guns, like *Robinfon Crufoe*, were all his OBI.; with which, and his courage in defcending into the plains and plundering to fupply his wants, and his fkill in retreating into difficult faftneffes, among the mountains, commanding the only accefs to them, where none dared to follow him, he terrified the inhabitants, and fet the civil power, and the neighbouring militia

* He was flain on Saturday 27th of January, 1781.

of that iſland, at defiance, for nearly two years.

He had neither accomplice, nor aſſociate. There were a few runaway negroes in the woods near Mount Lebanus, the place of his retreat; but he had croſſed their foreheads with ſome of the magic in his horn, and they could not betray him. But he truſted no one. He ſcorned aſſiſtance. He aſcended above SPARTACUS. He robbed alone; fought all his battles alone; and always killed his purſuers.

By his magic, he was not only the dread of the negroes, but there were many white people, who believed he was poſſeſſed of ſome ſupernatural power.

In hot climates females marry very young; and often with great diſparity of age. Here JACK was the author of many troubles:—for ſeveral matches proved unhappy.

"Give a dog an ill name, and hang him."

Clamours roſe on clamours againſt the cruel ſorcerer; and every conjugal miſhap was laid at the door of JACK's malific ſpell of *tying the point*, on the wedding day.

GOD knows, poor JACK had ſins enough of his own to carry, without loading him with the ſins of others. He would ſooner have made a *Medean* cauldron for the whole iſland, than

than disturb one lady's happiness. He had many opportunities; and, though he had a mortal hatred to white men, he was never known to hurt a child, or abuse a woman.

But even JACK himself was born to die.

Allured by the rewards offered by Governor DALLING, in proclamations, dated the 12th of December, 1780, and 13th of January, 1781 *; and, by a resolution of the House of Assem-

* BY THE KING. A PROCLAMATION.

Whereas we have been informed by our House of Assembly of this our Island of Jamaica, that a very desperate gang of Negro Slaves, headed by a Negro Man Slave called and known by the name of *Three-fingered* JACK, hath, for many months past, committed many robberies, and carried off many Negro and other Slaves on the Windward roads into the woods, and hath also committed several murders; and that repeated parties have been fitted out and sent against the said *Three-fingered* JACK, and his said gang, who have returned without being able to apprehend the said Negro, or to prevent his making head again: And whereas our said House of Assembly hath requested us to give directions for issuing a Proclamation, offering a reward for apprehending the said Negro called *Three-fingered* JACK, and also a further reward for apprehending each and every Negro Man Slave belonging to the said gang, and delivering him or them to any of the gaolers in this Island: And whereas, we have since received another message from our said House of Assembly, requesting us to offer an additional reward of *Two Hundred Pounds,* as a further encouragement for the apprehending, or bringing in the head of that daring Rebel, called *Three-fingered* JACK, who hath hitherto eluded every attempt against him: We, having taken the same into our consideration, have thought fit to issue this our Royal Proclamation,

 hereby

Aſſembly *, which followed the firſt proclamation; two negroes, named QUASHEE, and SAM

hereby ſtrictly charging and commanding, and we do hereby ſtrictly charge and command, all and every our loving ſubjects within our ſaid Iſland, to purſue and apprehend, or cauſe to be purſued and apprehended, the body of the ſaid Negro Man named *Three-fingered* JACK, and alſo of each and every Negro Man Slave belonging to the ſaid gang, and deliver him or them to any of the gaolers of this Iſland. And we do, at the inſtance of our ſaid Houſe of Aſſembly, offer a reward of *One Hundred Pounds*, and at the like inſtance a further reward of *Two Hundred Pounds*, to be paid to the perſon or perſons who ſhall ſo apprehend and take the body of the ſaid Negro called *Three-fingered* JACK. And we do, at the inſtance of our ſaid Houſe of Aſſembly, offer a further reward of *Five Pounds*, over and above what is allowed by law, for apprehending each and every Negro Man Slave belonging to the ſaid gang, and delivering him or them to any of the gaolers of this Iſland, to be dealt with according to law.

Witneſs his Excellency, JOHN DALLING, Eſquire, Captain-General and Governor in Chief of our ſaid Iſland of Jamaica, and other the Territories thereon depending in America, Chancellor and Vice-Admiral of the ſame, at Saint Jago de la Vega, the thirteenth day of January, in the twenty-firſt year of our reign, annoque Domini one thouſand ſeven hundred and eighty-one.

JOHN DALLING.

By his Excellency's command,
R. LEWING, Sec.

GOD SAVE THE KING.

---

* HOUSE of ASSEMBLY, 29th December, 1780.

RESOLVED, that, over and above the reward of one hundred pounds offered by his Majeſty's proclamation for taking or killing the rebellious Negro called *Three-fingered* JACK, the further reward of FREEDOM ſhall be given to any ſlave that ſhall take or kill the ſaid

SAM (SAM was Captain DAVY's ſon, he who ſhot a Mr. THOMPSON, the maſter of a London ſhip, at Old Harbour), both of *Scots Hall* Maroon Town, with a party of their townſmen, went in ſearch of him.

QUASHEE, before he ſet out on the expedition, got himſelf chriſtianed, and changed his name to JAMES REEDER.

The expedition commenced; and the whole party had been creeping about in the woods, for three weeks, and blockading, as it were, the deepeſt receſſes of the moſt inacceſſible part of the iſland, where JACK, far remote from all human ſociety, reſided,—but in vain.

REEDER and SAM, tired with this mode of war, reſolved on proceeding in ſearch of his retreat; and taking him by ſtorming it, or periſhing in the attempt.

They took with them a little boy, a proper ſpirit, and a good ſhot, and left the reſt of the party.

ſaid *Three-fingered* JACK, and that the Houſe will make good the value of ſuch ſlave to the propri tor thereof. And if any one of his accomplices will kill the ſaid *Three-fingered* JACK, and bring in his head, and hand wanting the fingers, ſuch accomplice ſhall be entitled to his *free* PARDON, and his FREEDOM as above, upon due proof being made of their being the head and hand of the ſaid *Three-fingered* JACK.

By the HOUSE,

SAMUEL HOWELL, Cl. Aſſem.

Theſe

Theſe three, whom I well knew, had not been long ſeparated from their companions, before their cunning eyes diſcovered, by impreſſions among the weeds and buſhes, that ſome perſon muſt have lately been that way.

They ſoftly followed theſe impreſſions, making not the leaſt noiſe. Preſently they diſcovered a ſmoke.

They prepared for war. They came upon JACK before he perceived them. He was roaſting *plantains*, by a little fire on the ground, at the mouth of a cave.

This was a ſcene:—not where ordinary actors had a common part to play.

JACK's looks were fierce and terrible. He told them he would kill them.

REEDER, inſtead of ſhooting Jack, replied, that his OBI had no power to hurt him; for he was chriſtianed; and that his name was no longer QUASHEE.

JACK knew REEDER; and, as if paralyſed, he let his two guns remain on the ground, and took up only his cutlaſs.

Theſe two had a ſevere engagement ſeveral years before, in the woods; in which conflict JACK loſt the two fingers, which was the origin of his preſent name; but JACK then beat REEDER, and almoſt killed him, with ſeveral others

others who aſſiſted him, and they fled from JACK.

To do *Three-fingered* JACK juſtice, he would now have killed both REEDER and SAM; for, at firſt, they were frightened at the ſight of him, and the dreadful tone of his voice; and well they might: they had beſides no retreat, and were to grapple with the braveſt, and ſtrongeſt man in the world.

But JACK was cowed; for, he had propheſied, that *white* OBI would get the better of him; and, from experience, he knew the charm would loſe none of its ſtrength in the hands of REEDER.

Without farther parley, JACK, with his cutlaſs in his hand, threw himſelf down a precipice at the back of the cave.

REEDER's gun miſſed fire. SAM ſhot him in the ſhoulder. REEDER, like an Engliſh bull-dog, never looked, but, with his cutlaſs in his hand, plunged headlong down after JACK. The deſcent was about thirty yards, and almoſt perpendicular. Both of them had preſerved their cutlaſſes in the fall.

Here was the ſtage,—on which two of the ſtouteſt hearts, that were ever hooped with ribs, began their bloody ſtruggle.

The

The little boy, who was ordered to keep back, out of harm's way, now reached the top of the precipice, and, during the fight, ſhot JACK in the belly.

SAM was crafty, and cooly took a round-about way to get to the field of action. When he arrived at the ſpot where it began, JACK and REEDER had cloſed, and tumbled together down another precipice, on the ſide of the mountain, in which fall they both loſt their weapons.

SAM deſcended after them, who alſo loſt his cutlaſs, among the trees and buſhes in getting down.

When he came to them, though without weapons, they were not idle; and, luckily for REEDER, JACK's wounds were deep and deſperate, and he was in great agony.

SAM came up juſt time enough to ſave REEDER; for, JACK had caught him by the throat, with his giant's graſp. REEDER then was with his right hand almoſt cut off, and JACK ſtreaming with blood from his ſhoulder and belly; both covered with gore and gaſhes.

In this ſtate SAM was umpire; and decided the fate of the battle. He knocked JACK down with a piece of a rock.

When

When the lion fell, the two tigers got upon him, and beat his brains out with ſtones.

The little boy ſoon after found his way to them. He had a cutlaſs, with which they cut off JACK's head, and THREE-FINGERED HAND, and took them in triumph to Morant Bay.

There they put their trophies into a pail of rum; and, followed by a vaſt concourſe of negroes, now no longer afraid of JACK's OBI, blowing their ſhells and horns, and firing guns in their rude method, they carried them to Kingſton, and Spaniſh Town; and claimed the rewards offered by the King's Proclamation, and the Houſe of Aſſembly.

THE

THE PLAGUE.

This word in the Engliſh, and its equivalent in every other language, takes precedency in the *Anaretic* vocabulary of medicine.

Λοιμος; *peſtis*, *peſtilentia*;—the plague, peſtilence.

Πληγη; *plaga*, *ictus*;—a ſtroke, a blow.

This *το θειον*,—this דֶּבֶר—this אַכֶּנּוּ בַדֶּבֶר "*I will ſmite them with the peſtilence* *,—is now as little known, as it was when Jehovah firſt delivered that terrible ſentence againſt the diſcontented followers of Moſes and Aaron.

Modern noſologiſts have gone no further, in general, than to obſerve that the plague is a

* Engliſh Bible, Numbers, c. xiv. v. 12. The LXX tranſlate this paſſage Παταξω αυτους θανατῳ. This is not right; דֶּבֶר cannot be rendered θανατος, *death.* דָּבַר he ſpake:—a word. The word of God's wrath. מִדְבָּר a deſart,—an effect from the plague.

fever, the leading features of which, are exanthemata, purple ſpots, bubo, and anthrax.

This definition, I conceive, belongs only to a ſpecies, or rather, to a particular condition, of this diſeaſe.

Hiſtory ſays the plague is generally the laſt act, in thoſe deep tragedies, bloody wars; famine; great and diſtreſſing mutations in the ſeaſons of the year;—and violent convulſions among mankind.

If that be true, this long abſent viſitor may ſoon return to many parts of Europe; and prove again an unwelcome gueſt.

Beſides, the intercourſe which the preſent times promiſe to eſtabliſh with Eaſtern countries, where the plague is a native inhabitant, is a new conſideration for Europe.

The philoſopher, the merchant, the ſoldier, and ſailor, are likely to become familiar with thoſe long-interdicted regions.

On this account, as well as to guard our great commercial city againſt ſurprize, and impoſture,—and not as a mere ſpeculation on a diſeaſe that gives us no concern at preſent,—I have brought the ſubject before the publick.

In North America, lately, her wounds, from a long and ſanguinary conflict, ſcarcely healed, the plague has burſt on the inhabitants.

It

It firſt appeared at Philadelphia in Auguſt, 1793.

I have lately read, that this "*Yellow Fever* viſited Philadelphia in 1760; and that it was then traced to have ariſen from the clothes of a young man who died in Jamaica, which were ſent to his friends in Philadelphia. His friends were the firſt who died of it; and though it extended to others, its ravages were not very extenſive."

I beg leave to remark on this aſſertion, that the *Yellow Fever* was not in Jamaica in 1760.

The *Yellow Fever* has reviſited Philadelphia, and appeared in ſeveral other towns in America repeatedly, ſince the year 1793.

The ſeaſon of its raging in America has always been in the months of Auguſt, September, October, and November; and from the 1ſt of Auguſt to the 10th of November, in 1793, the deaths at Philadelphia altogether, were 4041; and in the ſame period, in 1798—3506. At New York, in 1795—732. In 1798—2086;—all in the ſame period. The ſtatement of the deaths in 1798, at New York, was, that 329 died in the month of Auguſt, 1132 in September, 522 in October, and 83, up to the 10th of November.

The range of *Fahrenheit's* thermometer, during these four months, in 1798, at New York, was as follows:

		lowest.		highest.
August—	at sun-rise .	65°	——	79°
	at h. 2. p. m.	76°	——	96°
September—	at sun-rise .	40°	——	73°
	at h. 2. p. m.	52°	——	82°
October—	at sun-rise .	29°	——	64°
	at h. 2. p. m.	38°	——	76°
November—	at sun-rise .	30°	——	38°
	at h. 2. p. m.	35°	——	53°

The transitions in the atmosphere were considerable on particular days. On the 9th of August the increase of heat from sun-rise to noon, was 20°; on the 10th of September 14°. On the 26th of October 22°. On the 7th of November 18°.

Doctor Benjamin RUSH, of Philadelphia, a physician of the most distinguished learning and talents, has given an interesting account of this calamity *. He has denominated this pestilence the *Billious Remitting Yellow Fever* of America; from its being accompanied by the direful complexion, and other pathognomo-

* On the *Bilious and Remitting Yellow Fever of Philadelphia* in 1793.

nics,

nics, which I have given of the *Endemial Caufus*, or, as it is commonly called, the *Yellow Fever* of the Weft Indies; and from its yielding, as he has fhewn, to the fame means I ufed in that fever, and have publifhed in my *Treatife on Tropical Difeafes*.

From the mortality that has happened, at different periods, from this *Yellow Fever*, fince its firft appearance in America, I am forry to conclude that no fuccefsful method of treating it has been adopted by practitioners, and univerfally agreed on.

It feems that America is now fuffering the fame fate which England formerly experienced; and that this American plague, like the plagues in England, will exhauft the infcrutable caufe which feeds its rage, and then will vanifh. England was relieved from the plague, without any general rational method of cure being adopted, or without phyficians knowing any more how it came, or went away, than we do when it will return.

It was natural for HIPPOCRATES, who lived in a country, where particular winds regularly produced certain difeafes, to attribute all epidemics to fome condition of the air, that was cognizable to our fenfes.

But

But SYDENHAM, who, we all know, was a ſagacious obſerver of nature, and thought with HIPPOCRATES as to the atmoſpheric origin of epidemics, yet he contended that there was ſome ſecret and unknown quality in the air, not reducible to demonſtration, by the diviſions and ſubdiviſions of theory, in which the Pandoran miſchief of epidemics lies concealed.

There are annual or ſeaſonal diſorders, more or leſs ſevere, in all countries; but the plague, and other great depopulating epidemics, do not always obey the ſeaſons of the year.

Like comets, their courſe is excentric. They have their revolutions; but from whence they come, or whither they go after they have made their revolutions, no mortal can tell.

All epidemics properly belong to either ſpring or autumn. When they break out in winter, or very early in the ſpring, they generally prove the moſt malignant and deſtructive. The ſame may be ſaid of autumnal epidemics, in regard to their premature appearance, in ſummer.

Vernal peſtilential diſeaſes, and plagues, terminate, or become mild, or quieſcent, in hot weather. Autumnal diſeaſes, in cold weather.

ther. The meafles and fmall-pox, when epidemic, do the fame.

The plagues of 1119, 1656, and feveral others in England; of 1348, in London *, and Venice; of 1709 and 1713, in Dantzig, Hamburg, and Stockholm; all broke out during the froft in winter; and moft of them declined with the fummer heat. Such was the cafe with the plague at Toulon, in 1720 and 1721; and fo it is with the plagues at Conftantinople, and Cairo, where they generally make their appearance in February, and difappear about the end of June.

No perfon ever knew the caufe of the *Sweating Sicknefs* in England in 1485 †; nor of its periodical returns in the years 1506, 1517, 1528, and 1551;—nor why it has never fince returned.

Not lefs extraordinary was that mortal *rot* which broke out among fheep in 1274, and raged during twenty-five years, and deftroyed almoft all the fheep in England. This diftemper, according to hiftorians, who muft affign

* It broke out in London on the 1ft of November this year. It is faid that 50,000 people perifhed in the fpace of a year, and were buried in one church-yard, called the Ciftercians, near the Charter Houfe.

† It firft appeared in England this year, on the 21ft of September, and ceafed towards the end of October.

a caufe for every thing, originated in one very large fheep which was brought from Spain, by a French merchant, into Northumberland *.

As little fatisfaction can be obtained concerning the origin of a fingular diftemper that broke out among fheep in Germany in 1552; which caufed them to fwell enormoufly, and deftroyed them inftantly. The country-people, who flaughtered fome of thefe infected fheep, were feized with anthraces wherever the blood of the fheep touched them; thefe tumours fometimes fpread and increafed, and, from their inveteracy, killed many people †.

What can be faid refpecting the caufe of the peftilential havoc among oxen in France in 1514 ‡?

Or of the canine madnefs, which raged, to that degree, in Jamaica in 1783, that many dogs on-board of veffels in the harbours, from Europe and North America, which were never on fhore, were attacked by it, and died in the moft horrible ftate of hydrophobia §?

What can be faid likewife of the origin of that murrain, which deftroyed in and

* Baker, Chron. p. 101.

† Wierus *de Præftig. Dæmon.* lib. 4. c. 30.

‡ Fernelius *de Morb. Univerfal.* lib. 3. c. 12.

§ Treatife on Tropical Difeafes, Ed. 3. p. 44.

about

about London, upwards of 100,000 cats in 1797?

Who can ſay how it happens, that one ſpecies of animal, and not another, ſuffers ſo ſeverely on theſe occaſions?

In diſeaſes, even of confined local production, we are often deceived by the ſemblance of truth.

Has any perſon hitherto a rational cauſe to aſſign for Agues in the hundreds of Eſſex; or the Bronchocele in Alpine countries?

What did PLINY know of the *Gemurſa*; or what do we know of the *Mentagra* *?

To look for the cauſe of an epidemic in the preſent ſtate of the air, or weather, when it makes its appearance, is a very narrow, contracted, method of ſcrutiny.

The cauſe of a peſtilence in ſummer may be in the changes which the earth, and conſequently its ſurrounding atmoſphere, underwent in the preceding winter; and from combinations, perhaps, far beyond our ſcope of thought, for years preparatory to its eruption.

In a new country like North America, where immenſe diſtricts of the ſurface of the earth, which from the creation never ſaw the ſun, have been expoſed, for agriculture, the air of

* PLIN. lib. XXVI. c. 1.

the country muſt have been impregnated from exhalations injurious, probably, to its ſalubrity.

The Americans are not to look for the cauſe of their *Yellow Fever* on dunghills, in rotten vegetable ſubſtances, and about the wharfs and neighbourhood of Philadelphia. Nature does not deal in ſuch commodities. She does nothing on ſo ſmall a ſcale.

This peſtilence has a far more expanded origin. And I verily believe, that their melancholy officers of health, avoiding what they call infected perſons, and putting marks on the doors and windows of an houſe where any perſon is ill, and ſimilar acts of charitable and good intention, only tend to frighten the people, and diſhearten them, at a time they ſtand moſt in need of fortitude *.

Expoſing the well-known umbrous *Pontini* marſhes, by cutting down the woods, which kept their foul vapours from being rarefied by the ſun, and borne away by the winds, produced great peſtilence in Italy.

The idea alſo of the American plague being imported from *Bulam*, or the Weſt Indian

* In London in 1665, during the plague, a large red croſs was put on the houſes of the ſick: with, "Lord have mercy on us." "Pray for us." This drove away all aſſiſtance. It could not be otherwiſe. It was conſigning them to the grave.

iſlands,

iſlands, or any other place, is repugnant to reaſon. I was told a ſimilar tale, when I firſt went to the Weſt Indies: that the *Yellow Fever* there, was imported in the beginning of the century from *Siam*. That it was a contagious, and an original putrid diſeaſe; and that bleeding was death. In my practice I proved the reverſe of all this.

The cauſe of peſtilential epidemics cannot be confined, and local. It muſt lie in the atmoſphere, which ſurrounds, and is in contact with every part of us; and in which we are immerſed, as bodies in fluids.

Theſe diſeaſes not appearing in villages, and thinly inhabited places, and generally attacking only great towns and cities, may be, that the atmoſphere, which I conceive to be the univerſal propagator of peſtilence, wants a commixture, or union, with ſome compounded, and peculiar air, ſuch as is generated in populous communities,—to releaſe its impriſoned virulence, and give it force *.—Like the divided ſeminal principles of many plants, concealed in winds, and rains, until they find ſuitable materials and ſoil, to unite their ſe-

* THORESBY ſays, in 1645, when the plague was at *Leeds*, in Yorkſhire, that the birds fell down from the air, in their flight over the town.

parated

parated atoms; they then aſſume viſible forms, in their own proper vegetation.

Diſeaſes originating in the atmoſphere, ſeize ſome, and paſs by others; and act excluſively on bodies, graduated to receive their impreſſions:—otherwiſe whole nations would be deſtroyed.—In ſome conſtitutions of the body the acceſs is eaſy, in ſome difficult, and in others impoſſible.

The air of confined places may be ſo vitiated, as to be unfit for the purpoſes of the healthy exiſtence of any perſon. Hence jail, hoſpital, and ſhip fevers. But as theſe diſtempers are the offspring of a local cauſe, that local cauſe, and not the diſtempered people, communicate the diſeaſe *.

I know it is thought otherwiſe by FRACASTORIUS, the inventor of contagion, and his followers †.

* The 93d regiment, deſtined for the *San Juan* expedition, which arrived in Jamaica in 1780, brought with them the gaol-diſtemper. All the men taken from the jails, died on the paſſage; or ſoon after their landing in Jamaica. No others were affected by it.

† Vidimus anno 1511, quum per Germanos Verona teneretur, exorta peſte, quo hominum fere decem millia periere, ex una veſte pellica, non pauciores quam quinque & viginti Teutones obiiſſe; uno defuncto alius induebat eam veſtem, & hoc alius, & alius donec monefacti è tot defunctis veſtem combuſſere." *De Contag. Morb. Curat.* lib. iii. cap. 7.—See *Treatiſe on Tropical Diſeaſes*, Ed. 3. p. 268.

Plagues,

Plagues, and peſtilences, the produce of the great atmoſphere, are conveyed in the ſame manner, by the body being in contact with the cauſe; and not by its being in contact with the effect.

If peſtilences were propagated by contagion, from infected perſons, the infection muſt iſſue from their breath, or excrements; or from the exhalations of the bodies of the diſeaſed.

In ſupport of the laſt circumſtance, the black Aſſizes at Oxford in 1577 has been often inſtanced by authors; and that the judges, jury, and attendants, were deſtroyed by the infection brought into the court by the priſoners. How could this be, when the priſoners were not ill themſelves?

Inſulating the ſick, and debarring all intercourſe with them, according to the doctrine of contagion, would bound and ſtop the ſpreading of diſeaſes.

This was tried at Marſeilles in 1721, without effect. The Capuchins, the Jeſuits, the Recollets, the Obſervantines, the Barefooted Carmelites, the Reformed Auguſtines, all the Grand Carmelites, the Grand Trinitarians, the Monks of Loreto, of Mercy, the Dominicans, and Grand Auguſtines, who kept themſelves ſecluded

ſecluded in their ſeveral convents, and took every precaution againſt all communication from without, periſhed equally with others, by the plague *.

The infection, if it were not in the atmoſphere, would be confined within very narrow limits; have a determinate ſphere of action; and none but phyſicians and attendants on the ſick would ſuffer;—and theſe muſt ſuffer; and the cauſe, and the effects, would be palpable to our ſenſes. Upon this ground, the precaution of quarantine would be rational. But who then would viſit, and attend the ſick, or could live in hoſpitals, priſons, and lazarettos?

I had occaſion to notice, in a former publication, what I have here repeated relative to the vigilance uſed in vain at Marſeilles; and alſo that RHAZES lived 120 years, and often practiſed in plagues; that HODGES remained in town and attended a multitude of ſick during the great plague in London in 1665; that KAYE was in the midſt of practice in the ſweating ſickneſs in 1551; and without any inconvenience. PROCOPIUS informs us, that during a terrible plague at Conſtantinople in 543, which almoſt deſtroyed the whole

* *Journal de la Contagion à Marſeilles*, p. 42.

whole city, no phyſician, or other perſon, got the plague by attending, dreſſing the ſores, or touching the ſick *.

The ſmall-pox, meaſles, yaws, and lues venerea, know no diſtinction as to habits of body. Every human being is ſuſceptible of their morbific infection.

The two firſt diſeaſes are truly contagious, according to the common acceptation of the word in regard to fevers; and there is no ſecuring any perſon againſt being infected, who comes into the impregnated atmoſphere of a ſubject labouring under theſe diſeaſes. Their infection, as well as that of the other diſtempers, may alſo be put, by inoculation, into the habit of the ſtrongeſt man, or the weakeſt child. This cannot be done from the American *Yellow Fever*; nor from the ſuppurated, glandular, or cuticular matter, of any other peſtilential fever.

This convinces me that bubo, and carbuncle, which we hear ſo much of in Turkey, and read ſo much of in our own hiſtory of plagues, ariſe from heating food, and medicines; or from a defect, in not bridling the vehemence of the diſtemper, by a reverſe method of treatment. Theſe ſuppurations contain no in-

* *De Bello Perſico,* lib. 2. cap. 22.

fection,

fection, and confequently are not the natural depofit of the morbific virus, feparated from the circulation.

The ancient writers on medicine, and indeed all others, which I have read, affert, that the operation, of whatever they affign to be the caufe of epidemical fevers,—is folely on the blood and fluids. This may be doubted.

The impreffions of the atmofphere, on the furface of the body, when contaminated, or deprived of vitality, like Eaft winds, are as perceptible, as the effects of approaching, or retreating from, a fire.

In the common order of peftilential fevers, they commence with coldnefs, and fhivering; fimply demonftrating, that fomething unufual has been in contact with the fkin, agonizing cutaneous fenfibility.

The fkin is covered with the extremities of fibres, nerves, and veffels;—thefe are in the moft expofed fituation, with the leaft power of refifting external injury.—Hence a deftruction, or a privation of their elafticity, and reftraining power, from a poifoned atmofphere. —And hence I conceive that the firft blow in thefe fevers is made on the folids; — the ftrength of the whole frame is thus proftrated in in a moment, and every nerve and muſcle paralyſed.

In a ſimilar manner, perhaps, the denſe and concentrated vapour, from the *grotto di cani*; the bottom of brewers porter vats; minerals; vaults; wells; and ſubterranean caverns, when drawn into the lungs, deſtroy their functions mechanically.

Sickneſs at the ſtomach, and an immoveable preſſure about the præcordia follow. Theſe demonſtrate, that the blood cannot pervade the extremities of the body, and that the quantity which ought to dilate through the whole machine is confined to the larger organs, and is crowding, and diſtending the heart, and central veſſels.

The reſtraining power of the remoter blood veſſels being deſtroyed, the thinner parts of the blood eſcape their boundaries; hence ariſes yellowneſs in the ſkin, in ſome climates:—in others, the extravaſated groſſer parts of the blood ſtagnate, forming black lodgements, bubo, anthrax, and exanthemata.

The object in theſe fevers, is to decide the conteſt between the ſolids and the fluids; and this appears to me to be only practicable, when ſpontaneous ſweats do not happily appear, or cannot be raiſed in the manner I ſhall preſently

presently mention, by a cooling regimen; and by draining the vital parts, by bleeding and purging, before the fluids have burst their confines, and dissolved their bond of union with the solids.—The next step is to regain the lost energy of the surface of the body, by exciting perspiration; and then of the whole system, by tonics.

When these things are not done in the first hours of attack, in pestilential fevers, and the conflict is not *extinguished* at once, attempting to extort sweats from the body, by heating alexapharmics, will do mischief;—and bark, wine, stimulants, and cordials, may be called on—like undertakers—to perform an useless ceremony.

I am well aware of the objections that have been urged against bleeding in pestilential diseases, by inexperienced theorists; and by people who do not make just discrimination.

Debility of mind, and body; no thirst, and nothing indicative of fever in the pulse, though not the ordinary method of attack, frequently occurred at Nimeguen in 1636, and also in London in 1665; and proved as fatal as when the disease came on with the most intense heat, unquenchable thirst, dryness and blackness

blackneſs of the tongue, and intolerable burning about the præcordia *.

In the former caſe, no perſon would think of taking away blood. Bleeding has ſeldom been fairly uſed; nor does any writer, excepting BOTALLUS, appear to have duly conſidered its operation, extent, and time of execution, in various diſeaſes †.

It is not a few ounces of blood, however well timed, and if not well timed bleeding ſhould not be performed at all, that will anſwer the end in the Yellow Fever, or in the Plague.

Here lies the miſtake of medical men in theſe diſeaſes; and hence the violent clamours againſt bleeding. Such people only reprobate bleeding in peſtilential fevers, who never ſaw it uſed in a proper manner. It has either been performed on improper ſubjects, or too late, or in too ſmall a quantity, and where the practitioner has ſtopped at one, or two bleedings, when five or ſix, or what I have often known, ten or twelve, ought to have taken place.

If bleeding be not the chief ſtaff on which we can rely, or ſome ſafe and immediate eva-

* DIEMERBROECK. HODGES.

† BOTALLUS, *Cap. 7. de curat. per ſang. miſſ.*

cuant, whofe operations can be directed finally to the fkin, and terminate in fweat—fuch as the *Vitrum Antimonii*, ufed in the manner, and with the precautions, by which I cured peftilential dyfenteries in the Weft Indies *, practitioners will be in an hopelefs fituation when the plague returns.

There never was any medicine hitherto ufed that has produced the fmalleft oppofition to the progrefs of this difeafe, either in the cafes of individuals, or in communities.—It has raged on, proved fatal, and difappeared. Who can expect to find a fpecific rapid enough in its operation for furious peftilential fevers, which fometimes deftroy in a few hours, and often without a fecond exacerbation ?

Drugs cannot travel through the veins and arteries like the lightning of the plague. Their creeping courfe only fuits the lingering fteps of flow, diuturnal maladies ; and chronical, lymphatic indifpofitions.

SYDENHAM, confiftently with his general principles, caught the idea of bleeding copioufly in the plague, and was impreffed with the foundnefs of the doctrine ;—but he durft not give full exercife to his genius.

* See *Treatife on Tropical Difeafes*, Ed. 3. p. 232, 233. 252, 253 ; and Gentleman's Magazine for the month of June, 1797, p. 461.

The

The prejudice in his time againſt bleeding in any diſeaſe was great, and the hot regimen practitioners were numerous and powerful; and he had alſo, by his abſenting himſelf from London in 1665, during the violence of the plague, made it neceſſary that he ſhould be cautious in his practice when he returned, as he had loſt a glorious opportunity of riſing above cenſure, and benefiting the world.

Beſides, his leaving the town at ſuch a time might make the reliance he had on his own ſkill ſuſpected. In defence of bleeding in the plague, he produces the names of ſeveral excellent phyſicians prior to his own time; among whom the admirable BATALLUS ſeems to have decided his determination.

During the civil war, the year he does not mention, I ſuppoſe it was in 1647, he gives an inſtance of its good effects among the troops at *Dunſtar Caſtle*, in Somerſetſhire; which account was given him by Colonel FRANCIS WINDHAM, governor of that Caſtle.

He ſays, "it happened at that time, that a ſurgeon who had travelled to foreign parts, was in the ſervice there, who applied to the governor for leave to aſſiſt his fellow-ſoldiers who were afflicted with the plague, in the beſt manner he could. This was granted. He took away ſo large a quantity of blood from every patient at *the beginning of the diſeaſe*, and before any ſwelling appeared *; that they were ready to faint, and hardly able to ſtand; for he bled them all ſtanding, and in the open air, and had no veſſel to meaſure the blood, which falling on the ground, the quantity each perſon loſt could not be known. The operation being over, he ordered them to their tents; and, though he uſed no other remedy than bleeding, yet of the numbers that were thus treated, not a ſingle perſon died †."

I ſhall mention the practice of another phyſician, the celebrated empirical Doctor Thomas DOVER.

He ſays, in his *Ancient Phyſician's Legacy to his Country* ‡, when he was at "the ſtorming of *Guiaquil*, under the line, in the South Seas, it happened that, not long before, the plague had raged there. For our better ſecurity, therefore, and keeping our people together, we lay there in the churches, and brought thither the plunder of the cities. We were much annoyed by dead bodies.

* SEPTALIUS, RIVERIUS, and ſeveral others, bled after ſpots, tokens, buboes, and ſuppuration of the parotids, with ſucceſs.

† *Oper. Univer.* Ed. 1741. p. 119.

‡ Ed. 8. pag. 100, 101, 102.

Theſe

Theſe bodies could hardly be ſaid to be buried; for the Spaniards abroad uſe no coffins, but throw ſeveral dead bodies one upon another, with only a draw-board over them; ſo that it is no wonder we received the infection.

"In a very few days after we got on board, one of the ſurgeons came to me, to acquaint me, that ſeveral of my men were taken after a violent manner, with that languor of ſpirits, that they were not able to move.

"I immediately went among them, and, to my great ſurprize, ſoon diſcerned what was the matter. In leſs than forty-eight hours we had in our ſeveral ſhips one hundred and eighty men in this miſerable condition. I ordered the ſurgeons to bleed them in both arms, and to go round to them all, with command to leave them bleeding till all were blooded, and then come to tie them up in their turns. Thus they lay bleeding and fainting ſo long, that I could not conceive they could loſe leſs than an hundred ounces each man.

"Notwithſtanding we had an hundred and eighty odd down with this diſtemper, yet we loſt no more than ſeven or eight; and even theſe owed their deaths to the ſtrong liquors which their meſs-mates procured for them.

"They had all ſpots, which in the great plague they called tokens; few or none of the Spaniards eſcaped death that had them; but my people had them and buboes too.

"Now, if we had had recourſe to alexipharmics, ſuch as Venice Treacle, Diaſcordium, Mithridate, and ſuch like good-for-nothing compoſitions, or the moſt celebrated Gaſcoigne's powder, or Bezoar, I make no queſtion at all, conſidering the heat of the climate, but we had loſt every man."

HODGES was of the old ſchool in phyſic. He was an enemy to bleeding. He was a man of little reflexion, and no genius. He purſued the beaten track of alexipharmicks, and heating medicines. In his account of the plague in London of 1665, though he had abundance of opportunity, he made no diſcovery. He loſt all his patients. The ſick who recovered with him, were indebted to nature;—a rough phyſician on all occaſions.—None but the ſtrongeſt-conſtituted people ever eſcape under her hands alone.

This fact was illuſtrated here.—Women, children, and weak, ſcorbutic people, all periſhed.

HODGES, however, did all the good he could. Like a brave mariner, though he knew

knew not the uſe of compaſs, or quadrant,—he plied the oar, or ſtood to the helm, in that tempeſtuous "ſea of troubles."

The Doctor, if he were not ſkilful, he was honeſt. He gave his patients what he took himſelf. He endeavoured to cure them by his own preventive.

The Doctor loved old *Sack*. Like the elder CATO *, he warmed his good principles with good wine.

He modeſtly ſays, "before dinner I always drank a glaſs of ſack, to warm the ſtomach and refreſh the ſpirits. I ſeldom roſe from dinner without drinking more wine. I concluded the evening at home, by drinking to cheerfulneſs of my old favourite liquor, which encouraged ſleep, and an eaſy breathing through the pores, all night †."

HODGES always went about the town with his apothecary; his conſtant companion and friend. Theſe two, in the courſe of their morning rounds, uſually viſited as many ſack-ſhops as patients.—They had great practice.

There was a different tincture of character in theſe gentlemen. The doctor was bold;

* "*Narratur et priſci Catonis,*
"*Sæpe mero caluiſſe virtus.*"—Hor. Od. 21. l. 3.

† *Leimologiæ*, ſect. 8.

the apothecary timid :—but they hunted like true Arcadians. The doctor entered the most infected houses without fear ; the apothecary remained behind in the sack-shop, waiting for the prescription. The doctor saw death as a subject of speculation. The apothecary speculated on life, and saw her in brighter colours, proportionate to the operation of the doctor's prescription :—I mean that which the doctor took himself,—"SACK, *middle-aged*, *neat*, *fine*, *bright*, *racy*, *and of a walnut flavour* *."

I have no doubt but that Sack was of great use to HODGES, while he kept within bounds, —for excess is destruction ;—and, as far as it acted as a gentle stimulus to his mind and body ; and kept them in such a state of unison, as to enable the mind to act without fear, and the body without lassitude.

This is the great prophylactic against all pestilential diseases ; and is effected by temperance, and calmness of mind ;—avoiding fatigue, and heating the body ;—a nourishing diet ; cleanliness ; proper cloathing ; and keeping the excretory functions in a regular performance of their offices.

* *Loimologiæ*, sect. 8.——HODGES, to the disgrace of thousands whom he had served, fell into extreme poverty, and died in jail in 1684.

Veteran

Veteran physicians in times of danger generally desert the field; intrench themselves far off, behind old books, and leave raw recruits to fight the foe; who, inexperienced in the tactics of physic, seldom escape the recoil of their own artillery; and fall with the patients.

Few people in such times are to be found, inclined to secure their souls, at the expence of their bodies; like father Francis GARASSE. This pious jesuit, in order to purchase the crown of martyrdom, obtained, by repeated solicitations, permission from his superiors, to attend the sick, during the plague at Poictiers in 1631. In this benevolent office, the virtuous GARASSE, to his great consolation, got the plague and died.

BAYLE says, in enumerating the particulars of his character, that "this last action of his was very fine."

In times of pestilence, the sick are always neglected. For this, many causes may be assigned. Self-preservation has superior influence to every other consideration. In the plague of 1665, it is supposed that one-third of the people who died, had no aid or assistance; and that the greater part of that number

ber perifhed in houfes fhut up, alone, and helplefs *.

The clergy at that time left their flocks to take care of themfelves; and it was common to fee written on the church-doors, "*here is a pulpit to let,*"—"*here is a pulpit to be fold.*"

At that period of our hiftory, there was a great deal of religion in England; and the people were much diftreffed at the defertion of the clergy.

Among the few of this order, that had zeal, or courage enough to remain at their pofts, was the celebrated minifter Thomas VINCENT, who in his *God's Terrible Voice to the City*, has given a very animated picture of that peftilence. Many facts which conftitute part of thefe obfervations on that dreadful event, are known but to a few people; and I hope will contribute to illuftrate that momentous affliction, one of the greateft England ever fuffered.

The firft perfon who was attacked, died in the parifh of *St. Giles's* in the fields on the 27th of December, 1664. The difeafe then remained quiefcent until the month of May following, and, according to the account rendered in to the

* Such was the devaftation of this peftilence, that grafs grew in Leadenhall-ftreet, Bifhopfgate-ftreet, Cornhill, Exchange, and Cheapfide. Bucklerfbury was free from the plague, being at that time chiefly inhabited by apothecaries and druggifts.

the government by the company of pariſh-clerks, with which Mr. VINCENT's exactly agrees, now before me, the progreſs of the mortality was as follows.

			Died.
Anno 1665,—May	-	from the 2d to the 9th - - -	*9
Ditto	-	from the 9th to the 16th - -	3
Ditto	-	from the 16th to the 23d - - -	14
Ditto	-	from the 23d to the 30th - - -	17
June	-	from the 30th May to 6th June -	43
Ditto	-	from the 6th to the 13th - - -	112
Ditto	-	from the 13th to the 20th - -	168
Ditto	-	from the 20th to the 27th - -	267
July	-	from the 27th of June to July 4 -	470
Ditto	-	from the 4th to the 11th - - -	725
Ditto	-	from the 11th to the 18th - -	1089
Ditto	-	from the 18th to the 25th - -	1843
Ditto	-	from the 25th to Auguſt 1 -	2010
Auguſt	-	from the 1ſt to the 8th - -	2817
Ditto	-	from the 8th to the 15th -	3880
Ditto	-	from the 15th to the 22d -	4237
Ditto	-	from the 22d to the 29th -	6102
September		from Auguſt 29 to September 5	6988
Ditto	-	from the 5th to the 12th -	6544
Ditto	-	from the 12th to the 19th -	7165
Ditto	-	from the 19th to the 26th -	5533
Ditto	-	from the 26th to the 3d of October	4929
October	-	from the 3d to the 10th - -	4327
Ditto	-	from the 10th to the 17th -	2665
Ditto	-	from the 17th to the 24th -	1421
Ditto	-	from the 24th to the 31ſt -	1031
November		from October 31 to November 7 -	1414
Ditto	-	from the 7th to the 14th -	1050

* St. Giles's in the fields 3; Clements Danes 4; St. Mary Weſtchurch 1; St. Andrew Holborn 1.

Ditto

		Died.
Ditto -	from the 14th to the 21ſt - -	652
Ditto -	from the 21ſt to the 28th - -	333
December	from November 28 to December 5	210
Ditto -	from the 5th to the 12th - -	243
Ditto -	from the 12th to the 19th - -	68

There were ſome deaths after this, making the total amount, before the end of the year, 68,596.

The hiſtory of plagues, and peſtilential diſeaſes, is an hiſtory of ſuperſtition, and credulity.

The Romans, after the overthrow of the Samnites, were afflicted by a plague. They ſent an embaſſy to Greece for the god Æſculapius, who was then worſhiped in Epidaurus, a city in the Peloponneſus, under the figure of a ſerpent. After a year's expectation the god arrived, to the great joy of the people, and the plague ceaſed. Superſtition then was at ſo great an height, that the Romans had no idea that the god came "a day after the fair."

On another occaſion they had recourſe to the Sibylline books; in which a paſſage was conſtrued, that ſome great crime had drawn down the wrath of the gods upon their republic. A veſtal was found guilty of incontinence, and to appeaſe this plague, ſhe was buried alive.

The

The city of Tyre had long been exempt from the plague, when ſurrounding countries had been ſorely afflicted by it. Maximin, the tyrant there, attributed this, during the former part of his reign, to his zeal in perſecuting the Chriſtians, and putting out the right eye of every one of thoſe whoſe lives he ſpared, in his dominions.

The deſtruction, and annihilation of the people of Baſilica (antient Sicyon), by a plague, was ſaid by the Chriſtians to have been occaſioned, from the Turks reading the Koran, for the firſt time, in a church, which theſe infidels had converted into a moſque.

Nothing inferior to this, in human weakneſs, was the ſtatute 1. Jac. I. c. 31. ſect. 7. in England; by which ſick people going out of their houſes, who were ordered to keep at home, if they had no ſores on them, were puniſhed only as vagrants; but if they had any ſores, it was felony!

In 1665, it was ſaid that a globe of fire was ſeen over the part of the London where the ſolemn league and covenant was burnt; and that this was the cauſe of the plague. Some charged it to the reign of the Stewarts. Others attributed it to planetary influence, particularly to the effects of the great conjunction

junction of Saturn and Jupiter, which happened in fourteen degrees of Sagittarius, on the 10th of October, 1663 *.

Solomon Eagle, a well-known fanatical mad quaker, at that time, went about the streets naked, with a pan of burning charcoal on his head, denouncing the city of London for its crimes; and proclaiming every day, that the plague was not to end until the people were sufficiently punished for their wickedness.

* Ad hoc etiam causarum genus, aëris nimium vitium, referuntur *maligni syderum inflexus*, qui variis modis corpora viventium afficere consueverunt. Hujusmodi esse, aiunt, *coitum planetarum superiorum*, Saturni, Jovis, & Martis in *signis humanis*, qualia sunt. *Vergo, Gemini*, ac tum potissimum, cum Mars dominatur." &c.

"Cum enim morbi pestilentes saepe eveniant, nulla facta in aëre, quoad primas qualitates insigni mutatione; sed iis grassantibus aër purus admodum appareat, & purior interdum quam sub aliis constitutionibus non pestilentibus, neque praecesserint tempora admodum calida & humida, ex quibus insignes putredines solent exoriri; conjiciendum est, a maligno quodam syderum influxu morbos istos pestilentes originem traxisse. Adde, quod *pestes media hyeme* saevire soleant; quas nulla in primis qualitatibus insignis alteratio praecessit. Tunc enim *occultis syderum viribus* hujusmodi morbi assignandi sunt, cum vim habeant corrumpendi aërem, non facta in eo insigni aliqua mutatione, secundum primas qualitates. Et illud est divinum in morbis, quod agnovit HIPPOCRATES, & GALENO interprete." &c.

"Ad idem causarum genus referri solent, *luminarium defectus* & *eclipses*, *insolita meteora*, & prefertim *cometae*, qui nunquam apparere solent, quin morbi epidemici ac pestilentes, variaeque in mundo mutationes subsequantur prout multarum historiarum experimentis confirmatum est." L. RIVERIUS *de Febre Pestilenti*. Op. Med. Univ. Ed. 1679, p. 447, 448.

Others

Others prayed that all the quakers ſhould be ſent out of the land, and that nothing elſe could ſtop the peſtilence.

The nonconformiſts taking another turn, aſſerted, that after their firſt faſt day on the occaſion, "the Lord began to remit, and turn his hand, and cauſe ſome abatement of the diſeaſe:"—when it ceaſed, they fancied that their faſting had extinguiſhed it.

In recording this dreadful ſtory, ſome writers have ſolemnly affirmed, that there were marks, or tokens of the plague, on the walls of infected houſes, as mentioned in the Bible; and that theſe marks, or tokens, often broke out again on the walls, as they did in the leprous houſes among the Hebrews, "*with hollow ſtreaks, greeniſh or reddiſh* *," after they had been ſcraped and cleanſed away.

The ſame ſuperſtitions prevailed after the great fire of London, in the following year. On this occaſion, there was a wooden figure of Bacchus ſet up againſt the corner of an houſe in Pye-corner, where the fire ſtopped; with an inſcription on his belly, to acquaint poſterity, that the fire was a puniſhment for the ſin of gluttony in the city. The cauſe of this

* *Leviticus*, chap. 14.

ludicrous

ludicrous opinion was, that the fire began in *Pudding*-lane, and ended in *Pye*-corner.

In confirmation of what I have lately, and now ſaid, and what I many years ago advanced reſpecting contagion, and infection in peſtilential fevers, a very important fact reſulting from BUONAPARTE's expedition into Syria, in the beginning of 1799, has within theſe few weeks appeared, which will not be paſſed unnoticed by judicious phyſicians.

BERTHIER, in his account of that expedition, ſays,—" At the time of our entry into Syria, all the towns were infected by the plague, a malady which ignorance and barbarity render ſo fatal in the Eaſt.

" Thoſe who are affected by it give themſelves up for dead ; they are immediately abandoned by every body, and are left to die, when they might have been ſaved by medicine and attention.

" Citizen DEGENETTES, principal phyſician to the army, diſplayed a courage and character which entitle him to the national gratitude.

" When our ſoldiers were attacked by the leaſt fever, it was ſuppoſed that they had caught

caught the plague, and theſe maladies were confounded. The fever hoſpitals were abandoned by the officers of health, and their attendants. Citizen DEGENETTES repaired in perſon to the hoſpitals, viſited all the patients, felt the glandular ſwellings, dreſſed them, declared and maintained that the diſtemper was not the plague, but a malignant fever with glandular ſwellings *, which might eaſily be cured by attention, and keeping the patient's mind eaſy.

" He even carried his courage ſo far as to make two inciſions, and to inoculate the ſuppurated matter from one of theſe buboes above his breaſt, and under his arm-pits, but was not affected with the malady.

" He eaſed the minds of the ſoldiers, the firſt ſtep to a cure; and, by his aſſiduity and conſtant attendance in the hoſpitals, a number of men attacked with the plague were cured. His example was followed by other officers of health.

" The lives of a number of men Citizen DEGENETTES was thus inſtrumental of ſaving.

* DEGENETTES's views in making this diſtinction were highly commendable; but certainly this fever was the plague.

"He diſmiſſed thoſe who had been ill with the fever and buboes, without the leaſt contagion being communicated to the army *."

From the medical men of letters on that expedition, much more may be expected as to the treatment of the plague; and I underſtand that the world will ſoon be gratified on this ſubject by BERTHOLLET and his coadjutors.

Importing plagues,—like the exiſtence of contagion in peſtilential fevers,—is contrary to the opinion I ever had, and ſtill maintain.

From whence was the importation of the plague at Naples in 1656; by which 20,000 people died in one day?

Can any perſon, for a moment reflecting, believe that the great plague of London in 1665, which imagination traced from the Levant to Holland, and from Holland to England, was cauſed by opening a bag of cotton in the city, or in Long Acre; or a package of hemp in St. Giles's pariſh?

Is it poſſible to ſuppoſe that people ſhould have been found to propagate, or believe the

* Engliſh Ed. p. 83.

well-

well-known and favourite ſtory of the advocates for MEAD's theories,—that a lady was killed inſtantly by ſmelling at a Turkey-handkerchief; and a gentleman by only walking over a Turkey-carpet!

One might aſk—what became of the perſons, who delivered the handkerchief to the lady—and laid down the carpet for the gentleman?

How was the infection carried to the interior of Tartary, where it made its irruption on the world in 1346?

It is ſaid that this plague depopulated two hundred leagues of that country, and deſtroyed ſerpents, birds, inſects, and even trees. It ſpread to other parts of Aſia, and the Eaſt Indies; and into Africa, Egypt, Syria, Greece, and the iſlands in the Levant; and at length into every part of Europe, and continued its devaſtations, in different countries, for the ſpace of five years.

In 1347 it appeared in the Mediterranean iſlands, at Piſa, and Genoa. In 1348 in Dauphinè; and alſo in Catalonia, and other parts of Spain, and converted Florence into a deſart *. In 1349 † it invaded England; and, within the

* Vide BOCCACIO, *Decamerone, Giornata Prima.*

† It broke out in London in November, 1348. See page 213.

ſpace of one year, made almoſt a deſart of London.

In this year alſo, it broke out in Scotland, Ireland, and Flanders. In 1350 in Germany, Hungary, and Denmark. It is recorded that this five years plague, deſtroyed half the number of the inhabitants of the countries it invaded. This plague, the ſevereſt and moſt general in hiſtory, is ſaid to have originated in Tartary, from an intolerable ſtench which aroſe from the earth.

This is a cauſe of peſtilence much more rational than rotten vegetables, bales of goods, ſilk handkerchiefs, and Turkey carpets.

Earthquakes are generally ſucceeded by peſtilential fevers. The poiſon is thrown out of the earth, and contaminates the atmoſphere. Exhalations from the expoſed beds of rivers operate in the ſame manner.

In 1539 a peſtilence made great havock in England. There was a great drought that year. Moſt of the wells throughout the country were dried up. The beds of all the ſmall rivers, from the defect of water, were fermenting mud. The ſea water flowed above London bridge.

I have ſeen almoſt all the lazarettos, hoſpitals, and priſons in Europe. The worſt governments

vernments abroad, moſt abound with this ſplendid inheritance of paupers, and criminals;—the children of bad ſtate-parents.

Even in theſe falſe, cheating monuments of ſuperſtition,—theſe impoſitions on credulity and benevolence,—where pomp and magnificence are pictured without,—and neglect, dirt, miſery, and often malicious oppreſſion, found within, I never could diſcover that fevers are propagated by contagion. Were it poſſible ſo to be, I ſhould have been long ſince dead.

Quarantine, always expenſive to commerce, and often ruinous to individuals, is a reflexion on the good ſenſe of countries.

No peſtilential, or pandemic fever, was ever imported, or exported; and I have always conſidered the fumigating ſhip-letters, and ſhutting up the crews and paſſengers of veſſels, on their arrival from foreign places, ſeveral weeks, for fear they ſhould give diſeaſes to others, which they have not themſelves—as an ignorant, barbarous cuſtom.

Speaking thus decidedly, againſt the general opinion, and practice, I may poſſibly incur the imputation of raſhneſs, from the timid;—from thoſe who believe in their fears;—

and from ſome who adopt opinions on tradition, without examination.—But theſe are my ſentiments.—This is the way I take, to ſerve my country, regardleſs of the narrow notions of vulgar prejudice. For, from what has lately occurred in our metropolis, it is not difficult to foreſee, ſhould the plague, or any peſtilential fever like the plague, appear, how diſtreſs and miſery would multiply, through falſe alarms, miſrepreſentations, ignorance, and impoſition.

HOS-

HOSPITALS.

If plagues and peſtilential fevers were contagious, and generated from local materials only, independent of ſome diſpoſition in the atmoſphere, no populous city would ever be free from them; the Great Hoſpital at Naples, *di Santa Maria del Popolo*, or *Spedale Incurabili*, would furniſh ſufficient infection to contaminate the univerſe.

This hoſpital, ſo vaunted by the Neapolitans *, and ſo talked of by ſuperficial travellers, is the worſt-conducted hoſpital in Europe. It contains 1200 of the filthieſt beds I ever ſaw. The air of the wards is inſupportably offenſive; the floors, and the walls, are abominably naſty.

In ſuch a climate, theſe things are bad enough; but I wiſh this was all I could ſay

* Uno de' più magnifici Oſpedali d'Europa, per la vaſtità e magnificenza.

againſt this *grand* and *magnificent* building—ſo fair without, ſo foul within.

On this ſubject, I ſhall make only ſome curſory obſervations relative to the principal hoſpitals in Italy; as this country has lately ſuffered great changes, that future phyſicians may form an idea of the ſtate in which they were before theſe changes happened; particularly in the year 1787.

In this great *Spedale Incurabili* at Naples, there is a particular ward, where all the worſt caſes are indiſcriminately placed. Here are ſome dead, ſome juſt expiring, ſome in their perfect ſenſes, broken-hearted, calculating the minutes to their inevitable fate. Many are here alſo who might recover, with proper care, if all hopes of life were not extinguiſhed by the ſhocking ſcene before their eyes.

There were 138 inſane and idiotic people in appropriated apartments belonging to the hoſpital. The proportion of idiots was greater than I ever met with in any other country. Theſe mad people, and idiots, were all naked. The climate is no excuſe. The filth, ſtench, and wretchedneſs of their births, or cribs, conſtructed like thoſe of the wild beaſts in the Tower, exceeded all deſcription.

Among

Among the inſane, there was a boy about fourteen years old, who had not ſlept for three years; but raved day and night without ceaſing a moment, or ever cloſing his eyes.—I never ſaw, or read of, a ſimilar caſe *.

The treatment of the inſane here is very different from that which the inſane experience in Rome.

In the Great Hoſpital in Rome the *Spedale di San Spirito, in Saſſia*, there were at this time 816 patients, beſides 108 inſane, or fooliſh, on the eſtabliſhment. The inſane here are treated with the utmoſt ſkill and tenderneſs.

There is alſo every poſſible care taken of the ſick; but few recover. It cannot be otherwiſe, where people are ſo crowded together, in ſuch a climate, with low malignant remitting fevers; the produce of Rome, and the Campania. The wards are 45 feet wide, and about as many feet in height; much the ſame as they are in all the other hoſpitals in Italy. But the ſick are more crowded in this hoſpital than in any other. There are ſix

* Doctor Menghin ſhewed me an uncommonly reſtleſs mad patient in the Hoſpital at Inſpruck; who always either laughed or cried violently when ſhe was ſpoken to. Her inſanity aroſe from a ſudden ſuppreſſion of the menſes.

rows of beds in the wards, ranged head to foot, with a ſpace of three feet between each row.

There are many other hoſpitals in Rome; but this, and the *San Gallicano*, and the *Conſolazione*, are the principal.

The hoſpital *di S. Gallicano* is chiefly for the reception of people afflicted with the *Tinea*, or ſcalled-head; which is a dreadful diſorder in and about Rome. There were ſixty patients in the hoſpital when I was laſt at Rome in 1787.

The manner of curing this diſorder there, is curious, but extremely coarſe. I often viſited this hoſpital, and communicated my opinion of this barbarous practice to the learned SALACETI, the Pope's phyſician.

Their operators firſt cut off the hair as ſhort as they can; then pluck up by the roots, with a pair of pincers, the remainder, a little at a time, as the patient can bear the torture, until they have pulled out all the hair. They then ſcarrify the head ſlightly with a razor, or ſcalpel, and let out the blood, more or leſs, as they find occaſion. They finiſh the cure after this, with a cap beſmeared with oil.

The *Spedale di Conſolazione* is ſolely for wounds and fractures. When I was there, there

there were 50 men and 17 women in it. The Roman ſurgeons in this hoſpital, in all fractures of the thigh-bone, keep the injured limb ſtraight and extended to the length of the other, during the whole cure. They keep the limb in the ſame poſition in fractures of the patella. It is foreign to my preſent purpoſe to enter into a diſcuſſion on this practice; but they ſucceed better than the ſurgeons do in England, by their method.

The beſt-regulated hoſpitals in Europe are at Venice, Bologna, Milan, and Florence.

The military hoſpital of *San Servolo* is the only one in the Venetian territories under bad management. Here I ſaw men crawling about in the wards, with dyſenteries, and ſome dying in their beds, with heavy iron chains on their limbs. There were 40 inſane people in the hoſpital. The eſtabliſhment finds rooms and phyſicians for theſe inſane people, but their reſpective friends every thing elſe.

The hoſpitals in France, particularly the *Hotel Dieu* at Paris, and at Lyons, were at this time under much more ſalutary regulations than they were formerly; when it was a common practice to put four patients in

one

one bed, and frequently the dead, dying, and recovering, were lying together.

Thofe in Germany have undergone no improvement within my memory.

There is at Turin an excellent hofpital for orphans, and worn-out, helplefs, and aged people; the *Spedale della Carita*. There were in it 1800 females, and 1200 males, when I was there. The whole eftablifhment confifts of 3463 perfons.

The following account of the number of beds, and fick, in other hofpitals on the Continent, was accurate in 1787; and nearly the fame in 1783, 1785, 1786, and 1791.

Frankfort, 36 fick. Strafburg, 1800 beds, 205 fick in the military hofpital; the garrifon confifted of 8000 men; and in the town hofpital, 500 beds; 260 fick. Infpruck, 300 beds, 100 fick. Verona, 50 beds in the *Sancta Domus Pietatis*; 70 beds in the *Mifericordia*; and 1000 in the *Infantes Expofiti*. Padua, 140 beds. Venice, 160 beds in the *Ofpedaletto*; 35 beds in the *Ofpedale Dei S. Pietro e Paulo*; and 100 beds in the *Ofpidale di Mendicanti*. Bologna, 144 beds in the *S. Maria della Morte*; and 88 beds in the *S. Maria della Vita*. Rome, 200 beds, 137 fick in the *Incurabili*. Florence, 650 fick in the *Spedale di*

Santa

Santa Maria Nuova: the *Spedale di Bonifacio* was undergoing alteration, and had no patients in it then. Milan, 1400 in the *Spedale Maggiore.* Turin, 500 beds for the ſick in the *Spedale Giovani.* Chambery, 35 ſick in the *Hotel Dieu.* Montpelier, in the *St. Eloi,* 300 beds. Chalons, *ſur Saone*, 200 beds. Lyons, 900 ſick in the *Hotel Dieu.* Paris in *la Charitè*, about 300; in the *Hotel Dieu* 2611 ſick; there have been 5000. Lille, in the *Hôpital Général* 2500 people of all deſcriptions.

BRON-

BRONCHOCELE.

AT Turin I had an ample opportunity of examining a ſubject, long in my contemplation, on which there have been various ſpeculations and conjectures, among phyſicians, for many centuries. I mean the Alpine *Bronchocele*; or as it is called by the French, and in adjacent countries, the *Gouêtre*, and by the Germans, the *Kropf*.

In the hoſpital *della Carita*, there was ſcarcely one female, from the age of four or five years, to the oldeſt woman, exempt from more, or leſs, of it.

Among the males there were ſome affected; but few, in compariſon to the females.

Moſt of the womens' necks at Turin, particularly among the inferior claſſes of people, are enlarged. But here, as at *Chamberry*, becauſe their windpipes are not ſo compreſſed as to impede the articulation of their words, and

their

their necks not fantaſtically knotted, like diſeaſed trees with huge funguſes,—they think they are exactly what they ſhould be.

"*Quis tumidum guttur miratur in Alpibus* —* ?"

Phyſicians in general, have attributed theſe ſwellings to the rupture of the jugular veſſels, from drinking ſnow, and ice-water; ſome, to obſtructions, from the water being impregnated with mineral, ſelenetic, or other extraneous matter. The former has been the moſt commonly received notion, ſince the time of GALEN's comment on the *gongrona* of HIPPOCRATES; which diſorder, HIPPOCRATES ſays, is cauſed by exceſſive cold;—as ſnow, and ice †.

PLINY was of the latter opinion; and aſſerts that mankind, and ſwine only, are ſubject to this diſtemper ‡.

There are other curious opinions on this ſubject §.

It

* JUVENAL, Sat. XIII. v. 162.

† "*Frigidum valde venas frangit, & tuſſim citat, ut nix, glacies; & contrabit ut* pherea & gougronæ. *Simul cauſa duritiæ.*" Epidem. lib. vi. comment. 3. ſect. 14.

‡ "*Guttur homini tantum, & ſuibus intumeſcit aquarum quæ potantur plerumque vitio.*" Lib. ii. c. 78. Vide Lib. viii. c. 77.

§ "*Non ut pleriſque viſum eſt, ex immodicis clamoribus, aut ex potu aquæ ex liquefactis niwbus quæ in Alpinis aliiſque montanis in uſu eſt; ſed*

It is well known that the word *bronchocele* implies any ſwelling of the throat;—but there are ſo many ſwellings in this part, that the cauſe and treatment, of one bronchocele, muſt be very different from that of another.

The Alpine bronchocele is not the *gongrona* of HIPPOCRATES; nor the ſtrumous, ſcrophulous, glandular tumour of the neck, of modern writers.

CELSUS has defined the diſorder commonly received as the bronchocele, or wenn, better than any other writer *. But this is not the bronchocele of the Alps. The bronchocele of the Alps is, if I may ſo expreſs it, a paralyſis of the ſkin and tegamentous inveſtment of the neck and throat, with the cellular membrane; in which, the phenomena, conſtituting the tumor, is incloſed.

There are various popular notions as to the cauſe of theſe ſwelled necks, in every country, where they are endemial. The common people at Inſpruck, and other places in the Tyrol, believe they ariſe from a cuſtom, univerſal in-

ſed ex craſſa lentaque pituita, quæ eo ſenſim è capite ejuſque partibus externis per auris poſteriora devolvitur." FERNELIUS, de Extern. Corp. Affect. Pathol. lib. vii. cap. 3.

* "*In cervice, inter cutem & aſperam arteriam increſcit,* Βρογχοκηλην *Græci vocant; quo modo caro hebes, modo humor aliquis, melli aquæve ſimilis includitur; interdum etiam oſſibus pili immiſti.*" Lib. vii. c. 13.

deed among them, in theſe mountainous countries, of carrying heavy loads on their heads. But how ſhould this be the caſe, when this deformity appears in all ranks of people, from the cloiſtered nun, to the moſt expoſed peaſant? A phyſician at Inſpruck, a friend of mine, and his daughter, a young woman of eighteen, have both of them ſwelled necks.

In aſcending from Turin, to Mount Cenis, I ſaw many ſwelled necks; particularly at Rivoli, and between that place and Suſa.

The people here, thus affected, are very pale; many of them fooliſh;—dwarfs, with large heads, and wild countenance:—like the late, perhaps the preſent, celebrated Roman beggar, BAIOCCO, a well-known perſonage to travellers.

In deſcending from Mount Cenis into Savoy, ſwelled necks are ſcarcely to be ſeen at the town of St. Michel. Yet at St. Julien, the next village, there is ſcarcely a woman whoſe neck is in a natural ſtate.

If this bronchocele aroſe from melted ſnow, or vitiated water, theſe towns would be alike affected; the inhabitants of both, drink the ſame water;—that of the river *Arche*, which runs by all the towns and villages from the foot

foot of Mount Cenis, and falls into the *Iſere* near Montmelian.

At Hornberg, a town in the higheſt part of the mountains in the black foreſt in Germany, the women in general have conſiderably ſwelled necks; ſome of them prodigiouſly large, and deformed. The men have not. The young women's necks, though enlarged, are not ſeen to the enormous ſize of the more aged. I ſaw ſome *gouêtred* women here, with necks much larger, and more hideous, than the *monſtrous craws*, which were ſome years ago ſhewn for money, in the Hay-market, in London. Yet Hornberg is the only town, in that part of the black foreſt, where I ſaw any necks in this ſtate. But this is the caſe alſo continually in the Tyrol: in ſome villages it is hardly poſſible to find one woman without the *Kropf*, when in the next it is ſcarcely to be ſeen.

From the black foreſt, through Swabia, to the Tyrol, in the plains, the women are free from it; but they have bad teeth, which they never clean; and the peaſantry are eaten up almoſt with worms.

I have remarked that the right ſide of the neck is generally more affected than the left; and that when the neck is not lumpy, and irregularly ſwelled, or hanging down in flaps, or dew-laps, or protuding in knobs, the girls and women in general, in countries ſubject to this diſorder, have preternaturally large necks, downwards, and tapering conically upwards, from the baſe, at the thorax; as if aſcending, and ſpreading from about the thyroid gland.

From the preceding facts, it appears, that women are more ſubject to the bronchocele than men are: and that ſome towns are more invaded by it than others; though at the diſtance of a few miles only aſunder.

It is not common in high ſituations among the Alps. It is chiefly confined to the inhabitants living in valleys, and on the ſides of mountains; ſituations choſen for warmth, and which, in ſummer, are extremely hot, and in calms intenſely ſo.

Though the inhabitants in the higher ſituations in the Alps are not ſubject to ſwelled necks, their appearance is peculiar to themſelves. They look wild, have large foreheads, high cheeks, thin chaps, dark viſages, and long beards; conſtituting an harſh, but vigorous countenance. This ariſes from the poverty of their living, and the ſeverity of the climate repreſſing the ſofter parts of the fleſh, and exhibiting the prominent parts of the ſkeleton.

That

That women are more ſubject to it than men are, ariſes, I believe, not ſimply from the delicacy of their habits, but from their necks and throats being expoſed and open, from the manner of their dreſs, to the effects of the atmoſphere.

That one town, or village, and not another, in the ſame vicinity, ſhall be affected by it, is occaſioned, I believe, from the ſite, and aſpect of ſuch a town, or village; ſubjecting it to a current of wind loaded with frigoric particles, deſcending from neighbouring or diſtant mountains capped with ſnow, upon the inhabitants, heated and ſweating, in warm ſeaſons of the year.

In a journey from Milan to Turin, in the middle of ſummer, in very hot weather, I have had my lips and face chapped, and my nails brittle,—in the ſame manner as is common in ſharp froſts in England,—by the wind blowing from the North, from the adjacent Alps covered with ſnow, into the hot plains, where I was travelling.

Thus Inſpruck muſt ever be ſubject to the *Kropf*. The town ſtands under a mountain that ſhould defend it from the North; but it does not. The winds from that quarter are cutting and ſtrong. The mountains to the

Weſt are always covered with ſnow. The ſite, in ſummer, renders the town intolerably hot.

Moreover, I found that the popular diſeaſes in theſe bronchocele ſituations, are principally anginas, and pleuriſies,—and certainly from the ſame cauſe;—the ſharp mountain winds ruſhing on people living in heat-reflecting ſtations, and chilling their throat and lungs, when their bodies are hot, and perſpiring *. They are alſo much afflicted with red and diſeaſed eyes, and dropſies.

If I have directed ſome light on the cauſe of bronchoceles, it is all I deſigned on this occaſion. Much has been written concerning the treatment of ſtrumous, and other glandular, ſcrophulous diſeaſed tumours of the neck; but where the knife, or other means of extirpation, could not be applied, we read of nothing but a *dead man's hand*; *burnt ſponge*; or the *royal touch*.

The Alpine bronchocele is not to be conſidered as a diſeaſe; though it ſometimes proves ſo; by preſſing on the wind-pipe, obſtructing reſpiration, and cauſing ſuffocation.

As there is no poſſibility of removing the cauſe of theſe guttural affections, in Alpine countries, the beſt prevention is to guard the

* Derbyſhire, Glouceſterſhire, and Shropſhire, near the mountains, furniſh many inſtances of ſwelled necks.

neck

neck and throat with warm and defenſible covering, when the wind blows from any quarter, where it muſt paſs over frozen and ſnowy regions. Indeed, it is a faſhion among the peaſants in the Tyrol, particularly from Feuſen to Trent, to wear large rolled-up black handkerchiefs about their necks; and when they are clean, and dreſſed in all their beſt apparel, as they are on Sundays, this ſenſible part of their clothing looks very becoming.

Great is the miſchief in England, from neglect of warm clothing, every year, when Eaſt winds, fogs, and the moſt variable weather, prevail. In the laſt ſpring 1799, beſides an unuſual number of rheumatic, and paralytic caſes, and apoplexies, I do not remember to have ſeen, in ſo ſhort a ſpace of time, ſo many pulmonic diſeaſes, and rapid conſumptions; all ariſing, in a great meaſure, from the ſame cauſe.

PRISONS.

PRISONS may be confidered as emblematic of the character of governments ; or of the morals of the people.

When I was in Venice, I defcended into the cells of the *Prigioni Publiche*, or Great Common Prifon.

Here,—even here,—the foul of man clings to his body ; and fhews no more fymptoms, or prefcience of immortality, than if that body were on a bed of down, canopied in a gorgeous palace.

In the morning, when I fet out on this gloomy expedition, *Dominico Zacchi*, my Venetian fervant, who had before attended Lord *St. Afaph*, Sir *George Beaumont*, and feveral other Englifh travellers, during their refidence at Venice, took his leave of me. This was on the 16th of September, 1787.

Dominico thought I fhould never return ; or, if I did, I might "a tale unfold," that would endanger

endanger my ſafety at Venice.—But he ſaid, from what he had heard, he did not think it poſſible for me to ſurvive the foul and peſtilential air I had to encounter.

My deſign was to ſee the perfection,—the far-famed ultimatum of policy;—the immured for life, in *ſolitary cells*.

The late Mr. *John Howard*, F. R. S. was at the priſon when he was in Venice; but he only heard ſomething, and ſaw nothing, of this priſon of priſons.

He had not bodily ſtrength to bear the exertion required in ſuch an undertaking. Neither do I believe he would have been ſuffered to enter them. It was with ſome difficulty that I obtained permiſſion from the inquiſitors; which was granted me merely on account of my being an Engliſh phyſician; a character much reſpected at that time in Venice. I wiſhed to have ſeen the *Sotto Piombi*, where the ſtate priſoners were kept; but that was refuſed. Here, under the roof of the public buildings, they are confined; expoſed to the rigour of winter's cold, and ſummer's heat, and the viciſſitudes of ſcorching days, and chilling nights.

Paul Renier was then Doge; he, who married a Neapolitan dancer, when he was ambaſſador

ambaſſador at Conſtantinople; upon which account, according to the laws of Venice, his children were not *noble*; nor his wife qualified to appear at the great ceremonies of ſtate; nor to preſide at the entertainments given by him to the ſenate and nobility. He had been Doge nine years.

PAUL RENIER, thus circumſtanced,—as it might happen to an Engliſh Lord Mayor, whoſe wife had not her planets ſo well poſited as his Lordſhip, for acquitting herſelf in the vulgar tongue; or for drinking a bottle of wine, without an evil direction to her next neighbour,—was obliged to have his ſiſter, or his niece, to perform the honours of his table.

Had PAUL RENIER married the daughter of an Apothecary and Druggiſt, or of a Glaſs Manufacturer, or of a Silk Manufacturer, his children would have been *noble*; and his wife the firſt female in rank in the ſtate. It was chiefly by theſe three branches of buſineſs, that the winged Lion of St. Mark became ſo renowned in a magnificent, and once mighty empire.

I was conducted through the priſon, with one of its inferior dependants. We had a torch with us. We crept along narrow paſſages, as dark as pitch. In ſome of them, two people

people could ſcarcely paſs each other. The cells are made of maſſy marble; the architecture, of the celebrated *Sanſovino*.

The cells are not only dark, and black as ink, but being ſurrounded, and confined with huge walls, the ſmalleſt breath of air can ſcarcely find circulation in them. They are about nine feet ſquare, on the floor, arched at the top, and between ſix and ſeven feet high, in the higheſt part. There is to each cell a round hole, of eight inches diameter; through which the priſoner's daily allowance of twelve ounces of bread, and a pot of water, is delivered. There is a ſmall iron door to the cell. The furniture of the cell is a little ſtraw, and a ſmall tub: nothing elſe. The ſtraw is renewed, and the tub emptied, through the iron door, occaſionally.

The diet is ingeniouſly contrived for the perduration of puniſhment. Animal food, or a cordial nutritious regimen, in ſuch a ſituation, would bring on diſeaſe, and defeat the end of this Venetian juſtice.—Neither can the ſoul, if ſo inclined, ſteal away, wrapt up in ſlumbering deluſion, or ſink to reſt; from the admonition of her ſad exiſtence, by the gaoler's daily return.

I ſaw

I ſaw one man, who had been in a cell thirty years; two, who had been twelve years; and ſeveral who had been eight, and nine years, in their reſpective cells.

By my taper's light I could diſcover the priſoners' horrid countenances. They were all naked. The man who had been there thirty years, in face and body, was covered with long hair. He had loſt the arrangement of words, and order of language. When I ſpoke to him, he made an unintelligible noiſe; and expreſſed fear and ſurprize; and, like ſome wild animals in deſarts, which have ſuffered by the treachery of the human race, or have an inſtinctive abhorrence of it,—he would have fled like lightning from me, if he could.

One, whoſe faculties were not ſo obliterated; who ſtill recollected the difference between day and night; whoſe eyes and ears, though long cloſed with a ſilent blank, ſtill languiſhed to perform their natural functions, implored, in the moſt piercing manner, that I would prevail on the gaoler to murder him; or to give him ſome inſtrument to deſtroy himſelf. I told him I had no power to ſerve him in this requeſt. He then entreated I would uſe my endeavours with the inquiſitors to get him hanged;

hanged; or drowned in the *Canal' Orfano.* But even in this I could not ferve him. Death was a favour I had not intereft enough to procure for him.

This kindnefs of death, however, was, during my ftay in Venice, granted to one man, who had been "from the chearful ways of man cut off," thirteen years.

Before he left his dungeon, I had fome converfation with him; this was fix days previous to his execution. His tranfport at the profpect of death was furprifing. He longed for the happy moment. No faint ever exhibited more fervour in anticipating the joys of a future ftate, than this man did at the thoughts of being releafed from life, during the four days mockery of his trial.

It is in the *Canal' Orfano*, where veffels from Turkey and the Levant perform quarantine. This place is the watery grave of many who have committed political, or perfonal offences againft the ftate, or fenate; and of many, who have committed no offences at all. They are carried out of the city in the middle of the night, tied up in a fack, with a large ftone faftened to it, and thrown into the water. Fifhermen are prohibited, on forfeiture of their lives, againft fifhing in this diftrict. The pretence

pretence is the plague. This is the ſecret hiſtory of people being loſt in Venice.

The government, with age, grew feeble; was afraid of the diſcuſſion of legal proceſs, and of public executions; and navigated this rotten *Bucentaur* of the Adriatic, by ſpies, priſons, aſſaſſination, and the *Canal' Orfano*.

Mr. *Howard*, whom I before mentioned, whoſe leading paſſion was hunting after priſons, frequently ſaw no more than their anterior apartments; and ſometimes only the outſide of the buildings.

To reconcile the motives of this romantic perſon to a principle of benevolence, it is neceſſary to ſuppoſe he took into his conſideration only the corporeal contingencies of man; and that he was an entire ſtranger to the operations of the mind.

He knew nothing of experimental SOLITARY IMPRISONMENT; nor of the uſes made of that inſtrument, in thoſe terrible governments,—where intellect, and reaſon, are a misfortune, inſtead of bleſſing; where men, whom the Almighty has moſt favoured, are moſt dreaded; where legal inſtitutions are at war with nature; where the baſis of political ſyſtems ſtand on the perverſion of morals; and where the monſtrous ſuperſtructure is ſupported by training

ing man, like a wild beaſt, to make him the curſe and ſcourge of his fellow-creatures.

Roving about himſelf, unconſtrained as the feathered inhabitants of the air, *Howard* little knew the agoniſing condition of the compulſive ſolitary cell.

Buried in the grave, alive, as a commutation for a momentary death, how vain is the empty philanthropy of words; or the goodneſs of the marble, or the ſhape of the ſepulchre, in which "the beauty of the world, the paragon of animals," lies diſtracted on the rack!

If there be an hell,—the idea of which a virtuous mind can be ſuſceptible,—this is that hell; and ſome Italian devil was its inventor. Such a one, as he of that country, who, to accompliſh the eternity of the perdition of his enemy, beguiled him to diſclaim his faith, to ſave his life; then inſtantly ſtabbed him to the heart, to prevent his repentance.

What I now unfold, in regard to the priſon in Venice, is known but to a few people. I have reaſon to believe, that no foreigner beſides myſelf ever witneſſed the ſcene I have related; the exploring which, nearly coſt me my life.

The

The heat, and want of air in the paſſages among the cells, ſo oppreſſed my ſtrength and reſpiration, that I could ſcarcely walk, or breathe, when I left the priſon. Sweat ran through every pore of my body. My clothes were, to my coat ſleeves, wet through. I ſtaid too long there. I went to St. Mark's Place, as ſoon as I could; and, by the aſſiſtance of the trembling *Dominico*, waiting for my return, the bleſſed light of day, freſh air, and a few glaſſes of Maraſchino, I was enabled to get to my lodgings at the *Scudo di Francia*, on the ſide of the Great Canal, near the Rialto; where I was, for ſeveral hours, extremely ill, and for ſeveral days much indiſpoſed.

It is not my purpoſe here, to enquire whether the Venetian people were wicked, or the Venetian government wiſe; nor to ſettle the proportion of crimes and puniſhments, in ſuch a ſtate as Venice. An Engliſhman cannot.

But this *oculus Italiæ*, this proud virgin city, the idol of ſo many admirers,—"this model of human prudence, whoſe perfect ſymmetry had in itſelf no cauſe of decay or diſſolution *; whoſe dominion was, to termi-

* Harrington. Howell.

nate only with the world *,"—has deceived her prophets †.—Overwhelmed by a torrent of misfortunes, ſhe is now no more.

Reflecting on the wonderful exiſtence ſupported in the almoſt airleſs dungeons, or rather wells, in the priſon of Venice, not only under the earth, but under the water alſo (for one of them actually lies under the canal which ſeparates the Priſon from the Public Buildings ‡) for ſo long a time, to my aſtoniſhed faculties, toads living cloſed up in the center of ſolid rocks, and ſalamanders even in fires, did not appear incredible.

Bacon, indeed, aſſerts, that air is an enemy to life. But this doctrine has ever been conſidered as chimerical.

* "*Venetiæ non niſi cum rerum natura, et mundi machina peritura.*" Thuanus.

† Junctine, in 1581, with more modeſty, fixed the overthrow of Venice for the end of the next century. This renowned aſtrologer and aſtronomer ſettled the fate of this empire, taking the time when the firſt ſtone of the building of the city was laid; which was on the Rialto, where St. James's Church now ſtands, *anno* 421, 15th March, at noon. He decreed, "*Venetiarum Senatores domini ſceptra miniſtrabunt ad calcem uſque Virginei partus* 1880 *anni, vel circiter.* Vol. I. p. 816.

‡ The groans, and cries of people, have been heard at night, by paſſengers going up this canal in gondolas, under the *Ponte della Paglia,* by the priſon.

He

He ſays, " the excluſion of the air ambient, tendeth to length of life two ways; firſt, for that the external air, next unto the native ſpirit, (howſoever the air may be ſaid to animate the ſpirit of man, and conferreth not a little to health) doth moſt of all prey upon the juices of the body; and haſten the deſiccation thereof; and therefore the excluſion of it, is effectual to length of life.

" Leading the life in dens and caves, where the air receives not the ſun-beams, may be effectual to long life. For the air of itſelf, doth not much towards the depredation of the body, unleſs it be ſtirred by heat.

" Next to the life in caves, is the life on mountains; for, as the beams of the ſun do not penetrate into caves, ſo on the tops of mountains, being deſtitute of reflexion, they are of ſmall force. But this is to be underſtood of mountains where the air is clear and pure.

" And this kind of air, of caves, and mountains, of its own proper nature, is little or nothing predatory. But air, ſuch as ours is, which is predatory through the heat of the ſun, ought as much as poſſible to be excluded from the body *."

* Hiſtory of Life and Death.

BACON

Bacon founded theſe opinions from the hiſtories he had collected of the longevity of abſtemious ſecluded monks, hermits, and anchorites; men who wiſhed to live for ever.— He was unacquainted with the truth of his theory, in ſolitary cells, for the extinction of humanity.

He was himſelf ſo organiſed, as to be ſtrongly attached to life. He wanted "length of days;"—and had no idea that it is within the ſcope of nature to wiſh, and yet to be unable, to die. To count the painful hours, with increaſe of miſery, unleſs favoured by the viſitation of idiotiſm, or inſanity, and to languiſh for the arrival of the liberating hand of death.

Printed by John Nichols,
Red Lion-Paſſage, Fleet-Street, London.

For EU product safety concerns, contact us at Calle de José Abascal, 56–1°, 28003 Madrid, Spain or eugpsr@cambridge.org.

www.ingramcontent.com/pod-product-compliance
Ingram Content Group UK Ltd.
Pitfield, Milton Keynes, MK11 3LW, UK
UKHW042209180425
457623UK00011B/120

* 9 7 8 1 1 0 8 0 5 0 5 0 0 *